No-Fault Negotiating

A simple and innovative approach for solving problems, reaching agreements and resolving conflicts

Len Leritz

WARNER BOOKS

A Warner Communications Company

Warner Books Edition

This Warner Books edition is published by arrangement with the author.

Warner Books, Inc., 666 Fifth Avenue, New York, NY 10103

A Warner Communications Company

Printed in the United States of America
First Warner Books Printing: March 1990
10 9 8 7 6 5 4 3 2 1

Cover design by: Bob Cuevas

Library of Congress Cataloging-in-Publication Data

Leritz, Len.
No-fault negotiating : a simple and innovative approach for solving problems, reaching agreements, and resolving conflicts / by Len Leritz.--Warner Books ed.
p. cm.
Reprint. Originally published: Casa Pacifica Press, 1987.
ISBN 0-446-39104-2
1. Interpersonal relations. 2. Negotiation. I. Title.
HM132.L43 1990
302.3—dc20 89-70516
CIP

☆ How to deal successfully with these and other problem types: ☆

BULLIES, who threaten, demand, intimidate, and throw their weight around. Bullies say things like "I want it and I want it now!" . . . or "That's a stupid thing to say."

AVOIDERS, who hide, procrastinate, or refuse to negotiate for fear of losing. "I'll do it tomorrow" and "that's not my problem" are typical avoider tactics.

SCOREKEEPERS, who get what they want through manipulation. Their primary interest is themselves. "What is good for me is good for everyone" is a scorekeeper's motto.

PEACEMAKERS, who are nice guys, helpful Harriets, and people pleasers. They may say "We'll do it your way" —but there's often a price tag.

REBEL PRODUCERS, who often set out to prove they can do it themselves. They are independent tough guys who make tough negotiators: "What I do is my choice," "I'll show *you*," "Get lost!"

FIND OUT IN . . .

No-Fault Negotiating

"The more you use the No-Fault formula, the easier it becomes. Stressful confrontations evolve into rewarding opportunities."

—Jerre Maxwell
Senior Vice President, Sales & Marketing
The DiMare Company

"The No-Fault Negotiating process must have always been there, like gravity. It took Len Leritz to discover and redefine it to this clear and congruent presentation. And it works . . . like magic."

—Timothy E. Conver
President, Electronic Resources
Whittaker Corporation

Dedication

To Andy, Jay, Aaron, and Nicholas

ACKNOWLEDGEMENTS

I am grateful to the following people, each of whom made a significant contribution to the formation and completion of this book: Andre Auw, Jeff Smith, Marcia Witteman, Carla Perry, Catherine Gleason, Carol Angel, Ellen Oliver, and Merrily Enquist. I am also grateful to the many TEC groups and clients that gave me numerous examples and helped me refine my thinking and to James Fowler and Lawrence Kohlberg for their early work in developmental theory.

TABLE OF CONTENTS

PREFACE

THE NO-FAULT WAY

Would you like a magic way to always get everything you want, when you want it, from whom you want it? That possibility does not exist in the real world. However, following the principles of No-Fault Negotiating, you can get more of what you want, more often, from more people. You can get more than you need.

Effective negotiation is a matter of consciousness. It is being conscious about what you need and what you want others to do to help you get what you need. It also is being conscious of who the other person is and what that person needs to be able to cooperate with you. And finally, it is being conscious of the limitations and possibilities inherent in the situation within which you are negotiating (resources, time, organizational realities, etc.).

Consciousness creates options. Creating multiple options for getting others to cooperate with you in meeting your needs is the purpose of all negotiating. Helping you learn how to do this is the purpose of this book.

The No-Fault principles will help you:

- Turn resistance into cooperation.
- Get others to listen to and accept your ideas.
- Confront and resolve conflicts.
- Solve difficult problems.
- Manage and supervise others.

- Deal with problem people.
- Close sales.
- Collect delinquent accounts.
- Mediate disputes between others.
- Negotiate difficult contracts.
- Motivate others to take more initiative.
- Get what you want with a minimum of effort.

You may not think of yourself as a negotiator, but you are. No matter what you do, you are involved in negotiations every day. Bosses negotiate with their secretaries to get the work out on time. Secretaries negotiate with their bosses to give them reasonable lead time. Purchasing agents negotiate prices. Credit managers negotiate payment schedules. Administrators negotiate with their boards to agree on policies and long-range plans. Supervisors negotiate with employees to increase their motivation and improve their performance. Couples negotiate with each other and their children. City officials negotiate with citizens about locating a halfway house in their neighborhood. Professionals negotiate with clients to get them to accept their proposed designs, advice, and services.

Whatever your job, your success depends upon two factors. The first factor is your technical knowledge and skills. The second factor is your ability to get others to cooperate with you. This second factor, your skill at negotiating, will usually make the difference between high achievement and mediocrity—or even failure.

I choose the term NO-FAULT for the title of this book because of our tendency either to blame others or to get others to take responsibility for us. The objective of NO-FAULT NEGOTIATING is to get our needs met without someone else having to be wrong or victimized.

In No-Fault Negotiating, our objective is not to win or to "beat" the other person. Our objective is not to achieve a one-time advantage as if there were no tomorrow. Our objective is to understand what needs exist within ourselves and others and to find creative solutions which will respond to *all* the existing needs. It is a posture of understanding, of accepting real conditions and people, of mutual searching. It is a reality-based approach.

In No-Fault Negotiating, we realize that while we may be negotiating about objects or conditions or external problems—contracts, cars, curfews, money, quotas, procedures, facilities, policies, time schedules, production, performance—we are negotiating *with* people. We are negotiating problems *and* relationships. As No-Fault Negotiators, we realize that an essential part of our task is to keep the relationship in place while solving problems.

Section I describes the core concepts of the NO-FAULT NEGOTIATING theory: that the focus of all negotiations is to respond to human needs and that if you want to be an effective negotiator you need to be conscious of your assumptions.

Section II gives you a practical and detailed framework for interpreting and understanding behavior. You will be able to see through other's behavior and to respond strategically in ways that will make you a more effective negotiator.

NO-FAULT NEGOTIATING applies the latest structural developmental psychology research to the art of negotiating. Structural developmental psychology studies the different ways people think and relate at different ages or stages of development. Understanding how people think enables us to understand our own and others' behavior. Consequently, we have more conscious choices for thinking and behaving in ways that will get us our best results. The higher our level of thinking, the more powerful and effective we are.

Section III outlines four core principles to keep you in the highest levels of thinking. You will learn how to:

1. **CREATE A SAFE ENVIRONMENT** in which everyone remains open-minded and non-defensive.

2. **SHIFT YOUR FOCUS** so you know when to focus on problems, when to focus on relationships, when to focus on the process, and when to focus on the criteria for settlement.

3. **UNDERSTAND OTHERS** so your mutual and differing needs are clearly defined and you don't get stuck with limited solutions.

4. **ATTEND TO THE OBVIOUS,** your greatest strategy and tool for getting to the real issues and getting them resolved.

Section IV teaches you how to use the MAGIC NO-FAULT FORMULA—an easy five-step process that can help you be a superb negotiator. It will give you a practical guide so you always know what to do next.

Section V summarizes the key ideas of the NO-FAULT approach, and the Appendices give you several helpful tools for applying all the above.

The principles and strategies presented in this book have universal application. They will work in formal and informal negotiating situations. They will help you improve your business and professional relationships *and* your personal relationships with families and friends.

SECTION I

THE PRIMARY OBJECTIVE

CHAPTER 1

GETTING OTHERS TO WANT TO COOPERATE

The world is made up of little kids running around in adult bodies, doing the very best they know how to do to get what they need. And when they know how to do it better, they do so.

This chapter creates a framework for understanding how to more effectively get what you want from others. The framework is made up of three points:

1. *Five primary needs motivate most behavior in people.*
2. *Effective negotiators are people who have learned to listen on two levels—the obvious or content level and the insight or need level.*
3. *The core of effective negotiating is our ability to understand and accept ourselves, others, and the real situation we find ourselves in.*

NEGOTIATING TO SATISFY NEEDS

We find ourselves in the world with needs. Having needs is basic to the human condition. To be alive is to be needy. Homeostasis—having all of our needs satisfied and in balance—is death. Every time we satisfy one need, another need pops to the surface and grabs our attention.

When we feel bored or restless, we need a new and exciting challenge to get our interest. So we find a new project.

We don't feel bored any longer, but we feel anxious. We need to prove to ourselves that we can master the challenge; so we put all our energy into mastering it. We feel satisfied, but we're tired. We need to rest. We rest until we become restless, and the cycle repeats itself.

The human experience is an unending journey to satisfy needs. While we are all unique and different, we have the same primary needs. All negotiating is an attempt to meet those primary needs.

THE FIVE PRIMARY NEEDS

1. PHYSICAL SURVIVAL

We need to survive physically. We need food and shelter and rest and safety. Much of what we do in life is directed toward meeting our basic survival needs. We work to earn money. We get educated, join unions and professional associations, apply for tenure. We buy houses, make investments, take out insurance policies, save money and try to get to bed earlier (which never seems to happen).

If the other party in a negotiation does not believe his basic physical needs are going to be met, we are not likely to get that person's cooperation. If the vendor is facing loss of his business and doesn't know how he is going to support his family, his ability to cooperate is severely constricted.

2. WORTH/VALUE

We need to feel worthwhile, valuable, and lovable. We need to feel that we have a right to be here, to be alive, to be who we are. We need to feel that we have value for being who we are, just because we are. We need to feel that we have worth.

Our need to have worth and value is probably at the core of all our needs and all our negotiations.

The outcome of most of our negotiations are determined before we ever begin them. The outcome is determined by what we believe we have a right to have. It is only when we believe that we have a right to something that we allow ourselves to imagine or visualize ourselves attaining it. And it is only when we can imagine the possibility of it that we plan and act in ways that are likely to enable us to achieve it. If I believe I can or if I believe I can't, I'm usually right.

In all our encounters with others, we put a price on ourselves – a price on our worth. Sometimes we believe we are worth a nickel and sometimes a dollar. How much we believe we are worth determines how much we go for in a negotiation. Rarely does anyone give us more than we believe we are worth. How much did you sell yourself for in your last three negotiations? What criteria do you use to place value on yourself and others?

People do not take advantage of us; we only give ourselves away by undervaluing ourselves. On the other side, if we do not help the other person to walk away from the negotiation feeling respected and valued, then it is not likely that we are going to get that person's cooperation.

3. COMPETENCE

We also need to feel capable. We need to feel competent and adequate and strong. We need to know that we will be able to accomplish what we want to accomplish in order to get what we need. We need to know that we can get what we want from others when we need it.

What does this have to do with negotiating? Again, we get what we believe is possible. If we do not feel capable, we either don't try to get cooperation, or we tend to do it in a way that is not very effective. If I expect you to read my mind or if I criticize you instead of telling you what I want, it is not very likely that you'll pass the test. Then I can go off and say, 'See, I knew I couldn't get you to do it.'

The other side of this scenario is that we often falsely assume it is to our advantage to put others at a disadvantage in our negotiations—to have some kind of leverage over them. In some instances, lining up our leverage is the appropriate response. This is true if we in fact really cannot trust the other party. If they are trying to take advantage of us or beat us, we need to protect ourselves.

However, my experience is that we often set up or maintain this level of negotiating unnecessarily. We don't trust our ability to manage the negotiation successfully if we are simply open and honest and lay the facts on the table. Instead we believe we must withhold information or embellish the facts or they'll use our facts against us.

So we dramatize what happened and make excessive accusations and refuse to be accountable for our own behavior. We try to back others into corners and then wonder why they don't want to cooperate after we have embarrassed them or intimidated them or enraged them.

The way to get the union's cooperation is not by making the bargaining committee look impotent in front of its members. The way to get a customer's cooperation is not by withholding payment to squeeze some concession out of the customer.

Our job as effective negotiators is to make it as easy as possible for others to cooperate with us—not to see how difficult we can make it for them.

4. Belonging

The fourth group of needs that we experience all through our lives is our need to feel at home in the world. We need a place where our bones are comfortable. We need to belong, to know that we are accepted and not alone. We need to feel connected.

While we can do many things in life by ourselves, sometimes we need help. We need to know that we can count on others, that they will be there if we need them. And even if we can do it by ourselves, it can be easier and more fun to do it with others.

So we need others. We build and nurture ongoing relationships. We find others who can help us do those things we can't do or can't do easily for ourselves. We divide up the work. We establish agreements and contracts. Forming satisfying and useful relationships is the basis of all business and of much of our personal satisfaction in life. Negotiating is the basis of all relationships. *The degree of our success in negotiating is usually determined by the quality of relationship we have with the other person.*

5. Meaning/Purpose

We need to experience meaning and purpose in our lives. We need to be able to make sense out of life. We need to experience coherence and continuity and congruence. We need things to fit. We need a model or belief system through which we can interpret our life experiences.

We need to have a reason to get up in the morning—a reason to put on our shoes and go do it again. We need to feel as though the work we are doing is important, that it will make a difference, that it is worth all the headaches and long hours.

We need a sense of direction. We need to know what we want, where we want to go and how we can get there. We need road maps and charts. So we dream dreams and set goals and develop plans of action, and every time we get someplace, we start all over again.

But if what we are asking for doesn't make sense to the other person, it is not likely he will want to help us. *We need to make it easy for the other person to understand why we are asking them to do one thing and not another.* We need to make a case for our needs. People cooperate when it makes sense to do so.

Problems arise when we both need the same thing at the same time and it appears there is not enough to go around. A situation where two employees both want to take their vacations at the same time can be a problem. In other instances, we may each have different needs at the same time. You may want to talk while I need to get some work finished. That can also be a problem.

The consequence is that every day of our lives is a negotiating process. We continuously negotiate with everyone for what we need. We negotiate with our boss, our employees, our husbands, wives, and children. We negotiate with our clients, our banker, our insurance agent, our supplier, the sales clerk—with everyone.

How to Negotiate on Two Levels

These five areas of needs—to survive, to have worth, to be capable, to belong, and to have meaning in our lives—these are the stuff of life and of all negotiations. Not only do we find ourselves in the world with needs, we find ourselves in the world with others. We find ourselves with others who, like us, have the same needs.

ALL NEGOTIATING IS AN ATTEMPT TO MEET HUMAN NEEDS. These needs may be answered by getting the job, getting a raise, getting tenure, making the sale, agreeing to a fair price, settling the terms of the contract, motivating better performance, or changing the policy or procedures. But underneath all these solutions are human needs. Human needs are the substance of all negotiating. When we negotiate, we are negotiating with people—people who are doing what they are doing and taking the stands they are taking because the situation has some *meaning* to them in terms of their needs.

Being an effective negotiator requires that we be aware of human needs. It requires that we accurately identify the needs underlying behavior. This is as true in business as in other areas of our lives.

Learn To Perceive And Listen On Two Levels At Once

1. **THE OBVIOUS LEVEL**—the content or focus of the discussion (the contract, the lease, the price, etc.).

2. **THE INSIGHT LEVEL**—the underlying needs of the other party as symbolized by the solutions they are requesting.

For example, I may be negotiating with you to buy the family business which you started twenty years ago. You undoubtedly will come into the negotiations with a price in mind—the price you feel your business is worth.

If I'm a smart negotiator, I'll realize immediately that we are not just negotiating the actual market value of your business. If you started the business and it has your name associated with it, we are also negotiating your ego, your reputation, perhaps the security of your retirement, and whatever else the business means to you. The price and terms you demand for your business may well reflect not what its actual value is in the marketplace, but how much blood and sweat you've put into it, or your need to guarantee that your loyal longtime employees are protected, or that the quality of the product will be maintained.

Other examples are:

A supervisor complains about another employee's performance, but the real issue is that the supervisor does not feel adequately recognized for all he does.

A client resists participating in a staff development workshop, but the real issue is not that he is too busy and feels it will be a waste of time, but that he is afraid of receiving negative feedback from others.

The smart negotiator always negotiates on both levels—realizing that the real negotiation has to do with the underlying needs. *What the topic means to each person is the real subject of every negotiation.*

THE PRIMARY OBJECTIVE: UNDERSTANDING

As we come to understand the role of needs in our lives, we begin to realize that people are not good or bad, right or wrong. They are not greedy. They are simply needy. They are restless– –like us.

This realization is particularly important if we want to be successful negotiators. As long as we believe people are right or wrong, good or bad, we judge them. As long as we judge others, we believe we are in competition with them and we understand negotiating as a process of trying to win. We believe we must "beat" other people in order to get what we need. We assume that others are different from us and we cannot trust them.

We become lone warriors out to conquer the foe. We relate to others in ways that make them suspicious of us. As a result, they focus on protecting themselves rather than on cooperating with us. We block them from cooperating.

Whenever someone wins, someone else loses– –which creates more restlessness. The person who has been beaten, who has lost, cannot rest until he or she has gained back what has been lost. The victor is also robbed of rest. The victor must be watchful or he might lose what he previously won. All this watchfulness makes for a weary world.

The objective of negotiating is to understand. The objective is to understand what we need and what the other person needs. The objective is to create a cooperative relationship in which the other person helps us meet our needs and we help them meet theirs. If possible, each of us walks away feeling satisfied that we got what we needed. This way, we can each rest afterward.

NEGOTIATING IS A PROCESS OF CREATING MUTUAL UNDERSTANDING. It is not synonymous with being weak, giving in, or giving up. On the contrary, it means we do our homework so we are clear about what we really need or what the real problem is when we go into a negotiation. It means we listen to the other party and draw out the data we need from them to accurately understand their needs and problems and values. It means that we work at establishing what the real facts are so we can more appropriately and effectively relate to others in ways that will make them want to cooperate with us.

SECTION II

UNDERSTANDING THE OTHER PERSON

The objective in negotiating is to get others to cooperate with us in meeting our needs. In order to achieve that objective, we need to be able to understand others. We need to understand how they think and what makes them do what they do. We need to know how to interpret their behavior and how to melt their defensiveness. We need to know how to defuse the bully and counter the game player. We need to know how to avoid feeling obligated by the nice guy or dismissed by the superior type.

This section will take you a long way toward understanding others so you can get their cooperation. It describes five levels on which people function as they think and relate to others. In any negotiating situation, you and the person with whom you are negotiating will be operating from one or more of these levels. Understanding these levels will provide you with a practical framework for understanding the behavior of others and for effectively influencing that behavior.

CHAPTER 2

THE FIVE LEVELS OF THINKING

PEOPLE THINK DIFFERENTLY

As human beings, our levels of thinking range from the simple to the very complex. Persons who have developed more complex thinking abilities are better able to understand their own and others' behavior. As a result, they are able to build and maintain more effective and satisfying relationships.

To say that people think differently is a rather obvious comment, until you watch people negotiating. In the course of solving problems and resolving conflicts, we often seem to forget that people have different levels of thinking. Instead, we tend to believe other people think the way we think. If they don't, we assume they are stupid, or wrong, or obstinate—which is not always true.

THINKING DEVELOPS

The truth is that, as human beings, we go through a developmental process in our ability to think and to build relationships. We have long recognized that human beings develop and change physically throughout their life cycle—from the uncoordinated grasping of the infant to the agility and skill of the adult. The same type of developmental process occurs mentally in human beings—from the simple capacities of the preschooler to the complex, integrated capacities of the mature adult. This is a lifelong developmental process. It does not stop when we move into adulthood.

Human beings go through a sequence of levels or stages in the development of their capacities for thinking. The development of these capacities seems to occur in a universal manner in everyone. The more highly developed an individual is, the more choices or options that person has for responding to and interacting with the world and other people.

Thinking Explains Behavior

Understanding the developmental stages in a person's thinking is essential if you want to be an effective negotiator. When you understand the different levels and are able to recognize them in others, you can accurately identify the motivation and meaning behind their behavior.

You'll know how to defuse the bully and how to take the power out of the manipulator's strategy. You'll know when you are being conned and when people are simply doing the best they are capable of doing. You'll also know how to help others think and relate in more effective ways so they can give you what you need.

The levels on which we think and relate are not based on what we know or how much education we have. An individual may have a college degree but may be stuck in his or her developmental process and, as a result, may think on an Enforcer level. Have you ever argued with a highly educated person who acted like a preschooler—irrationally shouting and accusing or threatening you? Education does not prevent us from thinking and acting like preschoolers.

Different Thinking = Different Worlds

Each level of development represents a different posture or stance in the world. Persons on each level think differently;

therefore, they perceive and experience the world differently. Depending on the individual's level, he may experience the world as a struggle, a con game, a dependent obligation, a challenge, or a warm and abundant home. How people perceive and experience the world has a lot to do with what they do behaviorally and how they relate to others in negotiating for what they want.

Normal Range

Depending upon where an individual is in his developmental process, he will tend to function from one or two levels most of the time. Everyone has a typical norm, a familiar range of levels from which they will typically function.

Capacities Change—Children In Adult Bodies

You probably assume, especially in the business world, that you are negotiating with adults most of the time, if not all the time. Wrong. Just because the other person has gray hair or a three-piece suit or holds the title of President does not guarantee that you have an adult mind with which to negotiate.

Much of the time you are negotiating with children in adult bodies. The body may be forty-five, but the mind (level of thinking) is seven. And what counts in a negotiation is not the age of the body but the level of the mind. If you assume you are usually negotiating with adults, you are putting yourself at a serious disadvantage.

At the same time, levels do not remain constant. In a given situation, individuals will move in and out of various levels, depending on how safe or threatened they feel. The more threatening the external environment appears to them, the more they move down their levels of thinking. They get defensive. Their levels literally constrict, like a punctured balloon. The safer a person feels, the more his levels expand, like blowing up a balloon.

Clothes (and titles and educational degrees and age) do not make the man or the woman in a negotiation. Only the individual's level of thinking determines what kind of response you will get.

FIVE OPTIONS FOR GETTING WHAT YOU WANT

How skillful you are at negotiating what you need from others depends on your assumptions. Often, people negotiate from *Scarcity Assumptions*. The three *Scarcity Assumptions* are:

1. THERE IS NOT ENOUGH

The world is limited. There is not enough for all of us to have everything we want. We are afraid we won't get enough. We are afraid we will have to do without, compromise, give in, give up.

2. PEOPLE ARE GREEDY

Everyone is out to get everything they can for themselves, to line their pockets at our expense. We are afraid we can't trust others.

3. THE BEST APPROACH IS STRATEGIZING

Since the world is scarce and people are basically greedy, it logically follows that our best approach to getting what we need is to be more clever, to out-strategize others, to get 'ours' before they beat us to it.

If we base our approach to negotiating on these scarcity assumptions, then we operate primarily from fear. Out of fear, we feel impelled to try to control our world.

We have a variety of options for attempting to control our world. We can try to force others to give us what we want. We can strategize and attempt to trick others into giving us what we want. We can bargain and compromise. We can try the nice-guy approach and hope that others will feel obligated to give us what we want. We can dismiss others, show them that we do not need them, and be tough and independent.

These are the traditional approaches used in negotiating. Negotiating has been thought of in terms of rational problem-solving, strategizing, and bargaining to gain maximum advantage over others and of compromising when all else fails.

These traditional approaches have serious limitations. Even combined, these approaches will get us only part of what we want. They require a lot of energy and they hamper ongoing relationships. They set us up for unnecessary power struggles, and they limit our ability to develop mutually satisfying solutions.

Luckily, these are not our only options. We also have another option—to get what we want through *No-Fault Negotiating*.

No-Fault Negotiating is based on a different set of assumptions—The *Abundance Assumptions*. The three *Abundance Assumptions* are:

1. There Is More Than Enough

While the world is limited, you have always gotten more than enough. The obvious proof is the fact that you are alive. If you had not always gotten more than enough, you would be dead today. That does not mean that the world has been abundant for everyone. Nor does it mean that you have always gotten everything you wanted when you wanted it, from whom you wanted it. Life can be frustrating.

2. People Are Basically Needy, Not Greedy

People are not primarily greedy, they are simply needy. Whether you believe people are basically greedy or needy has a major impact on how you approach and relate to others.

To assume that others are greedy means that you begin from a premise of non-trust, self-protection, defensiveness, and non-cooperation. Since people have a tendency to mirror our reflection and match our behavior (I push against you, you push back), viewing others from an assumption of greed invites them to view us in the same manner and to respond to us from a posture of non-trust and non-cooperation.

On the other hand, by assuming that people are basically needy we are more open to identifying who the other person really is, and what he or she needs to be able to cooperate with us. We are more likely to realistically perceive the real person with whom we have to negotiate rather than act out of our own fears.

3. Understanding Is Our Best Strategy

The ideal situation is when other people want to cooperate with us by helping us get what we need. The objective of every negotiation is to get others to want (or at least be willing) to cooperate with us—to do what we want them to do.

Our task then is to create the conditions that will motivate others to want to cooperate. We can only do this, however, if we understand who the other person is and what they need. People are willing to cooperate when they are getting what they need.

But we can't give others what they want if the situation doesn't provide the resources or if we cannot afford it. I can't drop the price of your office lease by another 10 percent if that means I won't be able to cover my overhead. We need to create an environment of cooperation within the limits of real situations.

We have a variety of options for getting what we need. They can be divided into five basic approaches or styles. Each approach, which is also a level of thinking, reflects what we believe about ourselves and what we believe about others.

THE FIVE LEVELS OF THINKING

Basically, there are five levels of thinking: Enforcers, Scorekeepers, Peacemakers, Rebel Producers, and Generators.

1. **Enforcers** believe they must use force to get what they need from others. If they can't force what they want, they run away out of fear. Enforcers use threats, demands and intimidation, or avoidance and withdrawal. It is an all-or-nothing approach. This approach is characteristic of young children and adults who feel highly threatened or inadequate.

2. **Scorekeepers** believe that to get what they need they must trick or deceive others. They assume that everyone is out to line his own pocket and will take advantage of them if the opportunity arises. They are afraid of not getting their fair share. They are always planning strategies and keeping score to make sure they have not been cheated. Scorekeepers will use any kind of manipulation or gaming to get what they want. If their strategies do not work, they resort to bargaining and may attempt to achieve a 50/50 compromise. This approach is characteristic of the business community and of elementary school-age children.

3. **Peacemakers** believe that they must earn what they want by pleasing others, by taking care of others, and by not making waves. They believe they must meet others' expectations and that, if they take care of others, others will be obligated to take care of them. What other people think of them is important to Peacemakers. Their worth and value comes from earning the approval of others.

Peacemakers feel it is important to look good. They attempt to earn what they want by caretaking, pleasing, placating, accommodating, avoiding conflict, denying their anger, rescuing, and being appropriate. This approach is characteristic in our country of most adults and of the early teen years.

4. **Rebel Producers** believe that the best way to get what they need is to be independent and do it themselves. They believe the price of earning someone else's approval is too high, so they dismiss everyone and try to prove they can take care of themselves.

Rebel Producers act tough, push against traditional ways, challenge authority, work hard, do it all themselves, and feel impatient. Their mottos are "Show me," "I don't need anyone," and "Put up or shut up." This approach is characteristic of the late teen years, professional men in their 30's and 40's and, as a result of today's women's movement, many women.

Each of these approaches can get us some of what we need, but each approach has significant limitations. Enforcers wipe others out and eliminate the possibility of an ongoing relationship, or they withdraw and do not get anything. Scorekeepers can get results if they are good strategizers and hustlers, but their approach invites lack of trust. Peacemakers tend to have good relationships. Everyone likes them, but they continually give up what they need in order to please others. Rebel Producers tend to be productive and achieve a lot, but they have to do it by themselves and others feel dismissed by them.

In all these approaches, we function from a posture of scarcity. We are afraid we won't get enough. We are afraid we can't trust others. We are afraid others won't come through for us when we need them. We are afraid that we are not enough.

Fortunately, these are not our only options. We also have a fifth option—to negotiate as a Generator.

5. **Generators** believe there is more than enough. They believe that, despite the limitations of the world and other people, they can get more than they need. They believe that even though they have limitations they are still more than enough. They trust themselves and therefore they trust others.

Generators are generative in the sense that their self-trust becomes a source of intrinsic power and energy. They empower themselves because of their self-acceptance. Because they believe they are more than enough, they act as if they are more than enough. They are less defensive and more trusting. This, in turn, invites others to be less defensive and more trusting. As a result, Generators empower not only themselves, they also make it easier for others to function more pro-actively and effectively.

Generators believe that people are not right or wrong, good or bad—they simply have needs. They believe every person has a right to what he needs and that there is more than enough to go around. To get what they need, they attempt to negotiate with others to find solutions that will meet each person's needs.

It is only by behaving from the Generator level that we can really be effective at negotiating. Only Generators get what they need while maintaining satisfying, ongoing relationships. This approach is most characteristic of mature adults over the age of thirty-five.

How Generators Get More

Generators do it by using an approach called No-Fault Negotiating. In No-Fault Negotiating, the objective is not to win or to "beat" the other person. The objective is not to achieve a one-time advantage as if there were no tomorrow. The objective is to face reality and go from there. The objective is to understand what the existing needs are within us and within others and to find creative solutions which will respond to all the existing needs. The posture in No-Fault Negotiating is one of understanding and mutual searching.

No-Fault Negotiators realize that an essential part of their task is to understand others. They use multi-perspective, multi-level thinking to see the whole picture and to see through their own behavior and others'.

The motto for No-Fault Negotiators is that if they cannot understand others and help them meet their needs, they cannot expect others to understand them and help them meet their needs.

As No-Fault Negotiators, we realize that what another person needs is as much our problem (and opportunity) as his, if we want his cooperation. As No-Fault Negotiators, we attempt to prevent the negotiating process from becoming a competitive game or battle. Instead, we work toward making the process cooperative. Rather than set up a situation so everyone is planning their own strategies to beat each other, we attempt to get everyone to sit down on the same side of the table, to work together to solve mutual and differing needs.

We Match Each Other's Levels Of Thinking

We have the tendency to immediately match each other's level of thinking. If I push against you, you tend to push back (Enforcer). If I try to manipulate you, you become wary and strategize in response (Scorekeeper). And so on.

We can either get sucked into other people's ineffective levels of thinking, or we can draw them up to more productive levels that will get us both more of what we want. We can get drawn into a non-productive blame game or we can appropriately respond to other people so they quiet down and begin to own responsibility for their own behavior.

The choice is ours. Understanding the different levels of thinking will give us more choices in not getting dragged down into non-productive behavior.

The Name of the Game Is Options

As we move up through each level of thinking, we acquire more options for how we can get others to do what we want. Enforcers (like infants) either demand or go away (go to sleep, run away). Scorekeepers can do that but they can also employ endless strategies. Peacemakers can not only do what Enforcers and Scorekeepers do, they can also establish friendly, trusting relationships, obligate others into doing what they want, and use abstract logical thinking.

The point is that it is to our advantage to always negotiate from Generator capacities. From this level, we can do everything others can do and much more. We can use multi-perspective thinking; we can see through others' behavior; we can understand others without losing our sense of self; we can achieve results without getting defensive.

As Generators, we will use lower level behaviors not as a knee-jerk reaction to someone else, but because a particular behavior is the most appropriate way of getting what we want. We may aggressively confront someone not because we are

Enforcers and emotionally out of control, but because in considering the whole picture and all our options, we CHOOSE to be aggressive in order to get the other person's attention. It is an appropriate choice, not a reaction.

By negotiating from a Generative style of thinking, we lose nothing. Instead, we make all the options available.

Our objective in negotiating is to keep on the Generative level as much as possible.

CHAPTER 3

ENFORCER PROFILE

Style of Thinking:	Episodic. Intermediate. Fantasy-based.
Way of Relating:	Egocentric. Limited insight into others.
Core Need:	To Survive.
Key Emotions:	Rage. Terror. Confusion. Paralysis. Detachment. Emptiness. Hollowness.
Sense of Power:	Physical size. Visible symbols.
Behavior:	Compulsive. Impulsive. Aggressive. Withdrawing. Avoiding. Procrastinating. Hiding. Bullish. Pushing. Controlling. Demanding.
Beliefs:	Life is threatening. I have to protect myself. People who are

	bigger than me know more than me. I can't make it. If I withdraw, they can't get me. I have to use force to get what I want.
Style of Negotiating:	Fight or flight. All or nothing. Aggression or withdrawal and avoidance.

CHAPTER 3

ENFORCERS: GETTING WHAT YOU WANT THROUGH FORCE

You and I often encounter Enforcers in our negotiations. Sometimes we are the one in Enforcer level thinking. How do you know when you or the other person is an Enforcer?

Have you ever...

- Been in an argument with someone who refused to acknowledge your point of view?
- Felt like running away and hiding from someone?
- Felt enraged!
- Felt you were talking to a blank wall?
- Believed that someone was trying to punish you?
- Had someone make contradictory statements and be unable to see the contradiction?
- Confronted someone and found they kept disappearing, saying, "I don't know. I'll have to think about it."
- Had someone throw a temper tantrum?
- Had someone insist on having the last word or being right?
- Felt attacked?
- Been controlled by force?
- Been bored to death by a compulsive talker?
- Had someone refuse to negotiate with you?
- Been bullied?

- Assumed that someone bigger than you knew more than you did?
- Felt detached and gone numb to protect yourself?
- Felt helpless and powerless?
- Felt like you didn't have any choices?

ENFORCERS–WHO ARE THEY?

Enforcers are preschool-age children walking around in adult bodies doing the best they can to get what they need. For them, life feels urgent. They are afraid of losing everything. Therefore, they either come on like gangbusters trying to beat others into submission or they run away out of fear in an effort to protect themselves.

You can find them anywhere–among corporate presidents, factory workers, physicians, union members, lawyers, painters–anywhere you find people.

An example occurred in my family that illustrates this style of thinking. Several years ago, when my four sons ranged in age from four to nine years, I sat in the living room of our beach house and watched them aggressively wrestling out on the sand for a soccer ball. Suddenly, from the tangled knot of arms and legs, the ball popped out. My youngest son, Nicholas, grabbed it and went running down the beach knowing his life was in serious question. About twenty yards down the beach, he suddenly spotted a sand dollar and, forgetting that his life was in danger, stopped to pick it up. Bam! The army of urchins hit him from behind, leaving him flattened on the beach while they ran off with the prized ball. Nicholas dragged himself up, spitting sand out of his mouth, and headed for the house to get a hug from his ultimate source of power, me.

This scene characterizes what life is like for a person living out on an Enforcer level. The unquestioned assumption among my boys at that age, and at later ages, was that in order to get what they wanted, they had to use force. "You gotta fight for what you want or you won't get it." In that context, power was equated with superior physical size or strength. Power was also vested in me, their father, as a visible symbol of authority, who was even bigger. (I wish that were still the case.)

Negotiating over the soccer ball did not mean talking about it. The negotiating process boiled down to aggressively fighting or running away out of fear. It was an all-or-nothing situation. None of the boys were aware of what the others were thinking or feeling or needing, nor did they much care.

Nicholas' incident with the sand dollar was also a typical example of the Enforcer's limited capacities for thinking. He was easily distracted. His thinking was episodic, which means he was totally focused on the present moment, on the immediate stimulus before him. He was not seeing the whole picture. He was not thinking about the past (the fact that he was running for his life from his brothers), and he was not thinking about the future (the consequences of stopping to pick up the sand dollar). He was a prisoner of the present moment.

Being a preschooler, Nicholas' thinking process and subsequent behaviors were typical for his age. But we find these same behaviors in adults who feel highly stressed or pressured, including the alcoholic or drug abuser; the frustrated parent screaming at her kids; the overwhelmed husband who walks out and slams the door; the armed robber; the delinquent tenant who refuses to answer the door.

Enforcer Scenarios

We frequently find examples of Enforcer-type behavior in our day-to-day business interactions. Consider the following Enforcer scenarios:

Imagine yourself a corporate attorney in contract negotiations with other corporate attorneys. The sessions have dragged on into the second evening. Everyone is tired, and an attorney from the other side suddenly starts making personal attacks on your competence. You respond with counterattacks.

Imagine a graphic designer threatening to take her business elsewhere, if the printer doesn't get the job done by Friday.

Imagine yourself trying to get your business partner to talk about his anger with you. He refuses to say anything.

Imagine yourself being offered a challenging new project, and you keep putting it off because you're afraid of failing.

Imagine feeling depressed and overwhelmed and without any options.

Imagine yourself talking to your teenager about the job he left unfinished, and he explodes and accuses you of a long litany of offenses.

Imagine yourself making a presentation before a group of fifty businesspeople, and a man in the back of the group stands up, points his finger at you like Uncle Sam, and shouts, "You're wrong! You don't know what you're talking about!" (This particular behavior has a tendency to make you go numb and forget what you just said, which means he has just successfully pushed you down onto an Enforcer level with him.)

WHAT ENFORCERS DO

The common thread running through each of these scenarios is that one or both persons are either on the attack or withdrawing out of fear. The possible behaviors for persons in this stage of thinking are:

Insisting	*Overreacting*
Running away	*Not listening*
Avoiding	*Having the last word*
Disconnecting	*Being cautious*
Doing busy work	*Being invisible*
Throwing temper tantrums	*Being impulsive*
Compulsively talking	*Being insistent*
Avoiding decision-making	*Being abusive*
Locking onto one view	*Daydreaming*
Making contradictory statements	*Drifting*
All-or-nothing thinking	*Procrastinating*
Arguing	*Going blank*
Dominating	*Hiding*

Controlling
Pushing
Attacking
Denying
Demanding
Threatening

What causes people to act in these ways? The answer lies in their limited abilities for thinking. Because they think like preschoolers, they act like preschoolers. They have very limited options for making sense out of their experiences and for responding in effective ways.

HOW ENFORCERS THINK

Understanding how Enforcers think is essential if you are going to protect yourself from them or be able to bring them back when they withdraw. How do you know what's going on inside an Enforcer's head? Let me give you some clues. Enforcers think:

1. **Episodically**–They live in a series of unrelated episodes. They fail to see the whole picture or how things are related. They don't understand cause and effect relationships. They don't see that their yelling prevents cooperation.

For example, a division manager walks through his plant and sees two hourly employees standing by a coffee machine talking. Assuming they are wasting time and avoiding work, and without checking out whether they had a valid reason for standing there and talking, he angrily tells their supervisor to get them back to work and dock their pay. He also orders the coffee machine to be removed. Four months later, he is surprised to learn that there is a relationship between his actions and a 20 percent drop in productivity in his department.

2. **Immediately**–They cannot reverse the sequence of their thoughts. Consequently, they cannot tell you what they said five minutes ago. They cannot project into the future to assess consequences. They make contradictory statements and are unable to identify the contradiction. They are prisoners of the present moment.

For example, a neighbor says, "I couldn't pick up your newspaper because I wasn't home on Friday." And five minutes later he accuses you of parking your car in front of his driveway on Friday.

For example, an irate customer can't seem to understand why you can't deliver her furniture on Sunday and keeps making the same demand. After the third round, you stop her and ask, "Can you tell me what I just said?" Guess what? She has no idea.

3. **Unconsciously**—They react. They don't consciously examine alternatives. They will not be able to tell you what they are thinking if you ask. Life for them is a series of knee-jerk reactions rather than conscious choices.

4. **Based on Fantasy**—They confuse reality and fantasy. What they cannot understand, they fill in with their own limited fantasies. What doesn't make sense, they make up—and they can't tell the difference. They believe their own fantasies.

For example, your employee adamantly lies about why she didn't do a project and probably ends up believing her own lie.

For example, a traveling salesman has a flat tire on a country road. It's late at night and the longer he walks to find help, the more he convinces himself that no one will want to help him. He finally reaches a farmhouse, but when the farmer answers the door the salesman blurts out, "Keep your damn jack!"

5. **Projectively**—They lack any capacity for insight or empathy with others. They are limited to their own perception and are confused if someone sees the same situation differently. Unable to experience the feeling or needs or perceptions of others, they are unaware of the effect that their behavior has on others. Their world is the only one that exists.

For example, when the battle heats up between you and your spouse and she begins screaming that you aren't listening to her, she is not aware that her screaming is making it impossible for her to hear you.

6. **Emotionally**—Enforcers are frequently controlled or overwhelmed by emotions. Life feels urgent and pressing. They perceive situations in all-or-nothing terms. They find it difficult to wait or be patient. They are insistent. Their responses are

often infantile and inappropriate. They overreact. They make demands when a quiet request would be more effective.

For example:

I was conducting a seminar when one of the participants interrupted me in the middle of a sentence. In a charged, angry, demanding voice he erupted: "I don't want to understand him. I want to know how to beat that ——— when I see him this afternoon."

His statement was out of context and hostile and it confused me. I had no idea who 'him' was or what the meeting was about. I began to ask him. But halfway through my question, he interrupted me again, blurting out: "You're not telling me what to do. I want to know what to do."

At that point there was no longer just one of us in Enforcer thinking. His second interruption set off a red flare in me and I shot back, "If you would shut up for two minutes, I could give you an answer." It was time to take a break. I had just lost it.

7. **Egocentrically**—Enforcers experience only a limited sense of duty or responsibility. They cannot balance their own needs, interests, and rights with the needs, interests, and rights of others. Only their own self-interest has importance. Their motto is "Don't get caught." They judge the seriousness of an action by the severity of its consequences. Anything goes as long as they can avoid getting caught and punished. The primary question for Enforcers is whether they can get away with what they want without anyone noticing.

For example:

The chairman of a company is only concerned about the stockholders complaining. The contractor says, "If we don't use top grade materials, no one will know the difference." The business executive believes, "What they don't know won't hurt them. . .or us."

WHAT INTIMIDATES A BULLY (ENFORCER'S SENSE OF POWER)

From an Enforcer standpoint, power resides in physical size and in visible symbols of authority. Enforcers assume that people who are bigger than themselves have more power and know more.

For example:

The preschooler in each of us assumes that our big brothers and sisters know more than we do. I followed my older brother down many blind alleys as a kid. It was only when we were in our forties that I began to put him in realistic perspective. We had spent an afternoon in a fishing boat talking about investments and how much money we had made and lost. I suddenly realized, to my disappointment, that he did not know everything and when we stepped out of the boat onto shore, I was amazed to discover he was actually only two inches taller than I. Part of my little Enforcer had just grown up.

Enforcers also assume that persons who wear visible symbols of authority have more power and know more. Policemen, doctors in white coats, executives in three-piece suits, religious leaders in their liturgical garb—all are symbols of power and truth.

In the same manner, office location or size, the size of your house, the number and type of cars you own, how wealthy you are—all these are symbols of power for the Enforcer.

WHAT ENFORCERS BELIEVE

Given limitations in their capacities for thinking, it is not surprising that Enforcers have correspondingly limited beliefs about themselves and others.

Basically, they believe that life is a struggle for survival, other people are scary, they themselves are inadequate, and they must use force to get what they need or they must run away to protect themselves.

The following are common beliefs going on inside Enforcers' heads. (Please note that, while these beliefs will be the impetus behind an Enforcer's behavior, the individual in this stage will not be consciously aware of his or her beliefs.)

- I don't have any choices.
- No one will be there when I need them.

- You gotta bend 'em or break 'em to get what you want.
- It's OK to do it, if I don't get caught.
- I can't do it.
- I have to be demanding or hurt others to get their attention.
- I'm a failure, helpless, powerless...
- It's not safe to feel.
- I can never have what I want or need.
- All anger is threatening.
- I need to be invisible (hide) to protect myself.
- It's not safe to say anything.
- Get them before they get you.
- There is no one to take care of me.
- I won't be understood or believed.
- If I try to stand out, I'll be pushed back.
- I don't understand what is going on.
- There is one right way—my way.

Looking over the above list of beliefs, some repeating themes begin to emerge. I have summarized these themes in terms of common or characteristic needs of Enforcers.

Enforcers need to:

- Avoid getting caught.
- Avoid punishment.
- Avoid getting hurt.
- Be protected.
- Feel safe/secure.
- Have choices.
- Be drawn out.
- Not be left behind.
- Win or beat others.
- Avoid losing or being beaten.

Why You Do Not Want To Negotiate From An Enforcer Posture

When you identify your Enforcer beliefs, emotions, behaviors, and needs, you know when your capacities for thinking have been constricted. You know when an event or person has hooked into your early childhood fears. You know when you have given your power away and are least effective at negotiating.

Recognizing these same elements in others tells you when you are dealing with a preschool kid, no matter what the other person's chronological age or appearance. Responding to someone else's external behavior and assuming they should act differently because they look like an adult will sabotage your negotiations. *When an individual at any age operates from enforcer capacities, you are dealing with a kid, not a reasonable adult.*

We see the Enforcer in:

- The parent who forces his child to comply.
- The manager who intimidates her subordinates.
- The attorney who attacks his counterpart during a contract discussion.
- Israel's attack on Lebanon; Russia's takeover of Afghanistan; U. S. involvement in Central America.
- The contractor whose behavior threatens the building inspector.
- The union representative who throws a temper tantrum.
- The credit manager who threatens the delinquent customer.
- The partner who refuses to negotiate.
- The board member who always has to be right and have the last word.

If you are negotiating from an Enforcer posture, you will not be able to:

1. **Plan for your negotiation**, gather all your needed data, identify your needs and interests accurately, organize a set of strategic steps to take, or create alternative solutions.
2. **See the whole picture** and how each element and person is related, or weigh the relative importance of each element.
3. **Analyze the problem** by separating its elements and defining their causes.
4. **Think deductively or inductively**.

5. **Think consistently.**
6. **Understand the other person's perceptions** or behaviors or needs—why they have adopted their position and not yours.
7. **Make others feel understood**, safe, and cooperative.
8. **Adopt an objective**, third-person perspective to observe the process taking place between yourself and the other person and the quality of your relationship. Your awareness will be focused on the issue at hand and you will not see what is blocking you from getting what you want. You will not be able to separate the problem issues from the process or relationship issues and you will be easily sidetracked.
9. **Accurately assess your own and others' power.** You will falsely assume that individuals who are bigger than you or who wear visible signs of authority have more power than you do.
10. **Maintain self-discipline.** You will feel controlled and overwhelmed by your emotions. You will feel pressured and impatient and will act impulsively. You will be swayed by the emotional force of arguments and at times you will overreact and behave inappropriately and irrationally.
11. **Understand negotiating** as a search for mutually beneficial solutions. You will assume that negotiating is synonymous with winning and beating others. Your primary motivation in a negotiation will be to avoid losing, being "beaten," or getting hurt. Negotiating will be an all or nothing, fight or flight affair. Your behavioral options will be limited to force (pushing, threatening, demanding, being aggressive, attacking, etc.) or running away in fear (hiding, becoming invisible, emotionally withdrawing, physically avoiding, going blank, procrastinating.)

If these behaviors don't appeal to you, you still have four other options. But what do you do if someone is operating from an Enforcer stance? Detailed options are presented in the next chapter.

CHAPTER 4

TAKING THE BULL OUT OF THE BULLY

Negotiating would be easy if we didn't have to deal with problem people—if everyone would be reasonable and see things our way. The reality, however, is that much of the time we are dealing with problem people. Much of the time we are negotiating with people who look like adults on the outside but are thinking like kids on the inside.

ENFORCER TYPES: BULLIES, AVOIDERS, WITHDRAWERS, HIGHROLLERS, AND WADSHOOTERS

1. **Bullies**—Bullies will verbally or physically attack, use threats, demand or otherwise attempt to intimidate and push others around. Their basic approach is to use force. You hear them say things like:

   "That's a stupid thing to say!"
   "Do you expect me to respond to that?"
   "If you don't, I will. . . !"
   "I want it, and I want it now!"
   "Move it!"
   "You can't do that!"
   "You better shape up!"

We read daily newspaper accounts of Bully behavior:

- Bus Drivers Walk Out
- Tutu's Son Jailed for Insulting Police
- Nigerian Leader Overthrown
- TWA Airliner Highjacked
- Corporation Dismembered after Hostile Takeover

And we don't have to read the newspapers to find Bullies. They have a way of popping up in our own lives. A few years ago, one of my boys had a soccer coach who had a high need to win and who assumed the best way to improve athletic performance was by berating kids. He also assumed that no one had a right to question his style of coaching. I did... he showed up at my front door using the same bully behaviors. He wasn't able to hear me when I talked in a normal tone of voice. It required the filing of a formal complaint against him with the soccer board to get his attention.

On another occasion, I was representing a client in the dissolution of a business partnership. My client was tired of fighting and wanted to retire. His partner knew that and used it as a leverage to renege on an earlier agreement and to demand an additional $100,000.

In Response:

The first rule in negotiating with Bullies is that you have to get their attention. You have to draw a boundary of consequence. They need to believe that if they proceed on their present course, you will create negative consequences that will outweigh the benefits they hope to gain. You have to draw a boundary and you have to mean it.

Sometimes our tone of voice is enough of a boundary. When I say to you, "I will not tolerate your attempt to take advantage of me," and mean it, my words and voice tone may be enough to get your attention. Other times, tone of voice is not enough and we need to use stronger measures to get their attention.

In the previous example, we did a little research and found two important leverages. The first was that we found two prospective buyers for the business.

When we met with him again, we offered to buy him out based on the same formula he was requesting. At first he refused. We then hauled out our second lever, which was that the three key employees who made the business work had agreed to quit if he refused a reasonable settlement and would set up a competing business financed by my client. At that point, he committed to our earlier agreement. We had succeeded in getting his attention. This example also points out the importance of creating as many options as possible. *Your power is in direct proportion to how many options you have.*

2. **Avoiders**—Avoiders will physically avoid or procrastinate, hide out, or refuse to negotiate out of fear of losing. You'll hear them say things like:

   "I'll do it tomorrow."
   "We don't have anything to talk about."
   "I don't have time."
   "That's not my problem."

   In Response:

In negotiating with Avoiders, you must identify what their fear is and find a way to make it safe enough for them to stop running away.

My friend, Rob, had an office manager he needed to fire. After procrastinating for four months, he brought the issue up over breakfast one morning, saying that he had several major contracts coming up and a new person would not be able to cover all the bases quickly enough.

I invited him to do two things. One was to make a detailed list of all his performance requirements and find out from an employment agency how hard it would be to find a replacement. The second was to estimate what his manager's mistakes had cost him over the last six months.

Rob then came up with another concern. His manager had formed friendships with several of his key clients. He was afraid that it might damage him if he fired her. My response: check it out.

Rob did all three assignments and had a new person in place functioning at 30 percent better productivity within three weeks. So much for our fears.

3. **Withdrawers**–Withdrawers will emotionally withdraw, get confused, go dumb and numb, or become paralyzed with fear. You'll hear them say things like:

   "I don't understand."
   "That doesn't make sense."
   "I don't know."

   In Response:

The appropriate response toward someone who is withdrawing is much the same as with someone who is avoiding. Your task is to make it safe enough so the person does not have to withdraw or become confused. You need to ask yourself what it is that you might be doing that is contributing to the other person's fear. You may be closing the person down by your tone of voice, your persistent questions, your position in the organization, your threats, or your silence.

Some possible verbal responses might be:

"What is it that is confusing for you?"
"What don't you know?"
"What do you need to be clearer about this?"

4. **High Rollers**–High Rollers will attempt to shock and intimidate their opposition by making extreme demands.

   "You have until five o'clock to comply."
   "I want $50,000 for my car."
   "I want it all done by noon."

   In Response:

When responding to High Rollers, insist on fair principles or invite them to explain how they arrived at their position. Both of these strategies are explained in the next section of this chapter.

In Response:

"Can you tell me your criteria for that price?"

"I want to respond to your request, but I will need to do it in a manner that is also reasonable for me."

5. **Wad Shooters**—Wad Shooters assume an all-or-nothing, take-it-or-leave-it stance.

   "That's my bottom line."
   "If you don't want it, forget it."
   "Either you agree to all five points or I'm leaving now."
   "Take it or leave it."

   In Response:

Your possible responses are to ignore their statements, take a break, use silence, or insist on fair principles. All of these are described below.

What To Do With Them

Enforcer behaviors tend to be uncomplicated and obvious. Consequently, certain responses tend to work effectively with most Enforcer behavior. As we move into describing the upper or more sophisticated levels of thinking, we'll see that more individualized responses are needed.

The above examples of responses were brief. The following is a more developed list of useful responses for countering the various types of Enforcer behavior just described. These strategies will be carried out most effectively, if you are operating from the Generative style of thinking described in Chapter 11.

1. Get Their Attention

The first step in dealing with Enforcers is to get their attention. Until you get their attention you are wasting your time. Nothing constructive will happen until you do.

When you recall Enforcers' limited emotional capacities for empathy, you'll understand why it is essential to first get their attention. At this stage, you are not a flesh and blood person to them. You are simply an object to be eliminated, beaten, or avoided. Enforcers, being egocentric, are prisoners within their own bodies. *Who are you and what you need does not exist for them.*

Enforcers have no capacity to understand the effects of their behavior on you. To be passive or aggressive with them is nonproductive. To respond to them with aggression will scare them more and further constrict their ability to think. They will become more aggressive or more withdrawn. To respond passively will not get the Avoider's attention and will encourage Enforcers to push on since aggression appears to be working. To turn the other cheek to an Enforcer is suicidal.

Instead, you need to assertively get their attention. You need to shock them out of their self-centered stance and let them know that you mean business—that you intend to be taken seriously. You need to make them feel your presence.

You will get their attention by drawing a boundary. The intention in drawing a boundary is not to punish the other person. The purpose is simply to let them know what you will and will not tolerate. *The purpose is to create a negative consequence that will outweigh whatever benefit they are deriving from their current behavior.*

How you draw your boundary will differ in each situation. You need to ask yourself what it is that will get the other person's attention—what is important to them. You may do it by physical action, by shouting at them, by walking out, by filing for divorce, by initiating legal litigation, or by telling them in a quiet and firm voice what you will and won't accept.

The key to drawing a boundary is that you have to mean it. If you don't mean it, you're wasting your energy. The other person almost always knows whether you are serious in backing up your boundary. When you mean it, they know it. No one crosses your boundary when you mean it.

Here is an example of what I call the "Skillet Approach" to dealing with Enforcers. I once had a client who had been physically abused by her husband for years. On her part, she whined and nagged at him. When he couldn't stand it any longer, he'd let her have it. She had threatened to leave him for years, but he knew she didn't mean it.

One night she finally decided to mean it. He had pushed her around earlier in the evening. She waited until he went to sleep and then went to the kitchen and got her biggest cast-iron skillet. She woke him up while holding the skillet over his head. "If you ever hit me again, I'll kill you in your sleep," she told him.

This time she meant it and he believed her. Though he had trouble sleeping for a while, the abusive behavior stopped. The woman had gotten her husband's attention by creating a consequence (the skillet), and she meant it. She said it in a quiet, firm voice, not a whining nag.

Ask yourself what 'skillet' you need to use—and mean it when you use it. When you don't mean it, you are reinforcing the behavior you don't want. If you don't mean it, don't draw the boundary. And remember, if you don't draw the boundary, nothing is likely to change.

2. Explicitly Identify Their Behavior

The second step after getting the other person's attention is to explicitly identify the behavior and invite him to do something more constructive. Explicitly identifying his behavior will help him become conscious of what he is doing and will often take the power out of it. This is especially true if others are involved and the Enforcer feels embarrassed. Suggesting other options at this point will help him save face and will keep the negotiations moving. For example:

> "Your repeated attacks are not getting us any closer to an agreement. I'd like to suggest that we each try to explain what we need, then work together to brainstorm some ways that we might both get what we need."

3. Help Them Feel Safer

Help Enforcers feel safer so their capacities expand and they can move into more cooperative behaviors. You can help them feel safer by not becoming defensive and by looking behind their behavior to their underlying needs and interests.

"Would you be more comfortable if we met in your office?"

Respond to the needs in their internal kids, not to their external behavior.

"I can see how you feel frustrated."

Actively listen to them so they feel understood.

"What I hear you saying is . . ."

Help them create safe conditions by asking them what they need.

"What do you need to be willing to stay here and talk this out?"

Meet on their territory. Be aware of their constituency and to whom they need to look good.

"I want you to be able to go back to your department and feel proud of what we accomplished."

Above all, do not attack in return. Remember, the more aggressive the bully, the more frightened the internal kid. Helping bullies feel safer is usually the last thing you think of doing. And that's precisely what you need to do to get them on your level.

4. Insist On Fair Principles

Bullies, High Rollers, and Wad Shooters will attempt to force you to accept unreasonable agreements. When this happens, refuse to negotiate except on the basis of fair principles. Refuse to be pressured. Instead, insist on fair criteria for both the process and the final settlement. In getting their attention, firmly make it clear that you will continue negotiating only on this basis.

"I refuse to be pressured into an agreement. I am only willing to continue the negotiation if we can agree to some fair procedures that we will both honor."

"Let's check with some other suppliers and see what they are charging."

"The bluebook price for my car is $400 higher. I want to trade cars, but I am not willing to accept an unfair price for my car."

5. Invite Them To Explain

When the other person takes extreme stands and makes extreme demands, ask them to explain how they arrived at their position. Point out that you need to better understand their underlying needs. This strategy throws the ball back to them to justify themselves and allows them to be heard. Demands that cannot reasonably be justified lose their power.

"In order to understand your demands, I need to hear more from you about how you arrived at those points."

"Your price is a little higher than I expected. I want to pay you fairly for your work. Explain to me what you will need to do to complete the job."

6. Use Silence

Silence can be one of your most powerful strategies. When the other person is being aggressive or unreasonable, don't respond verbally. Just sit there and look at them calmly. Silence gives them nothing to push against. Calm silence communicates power. The other person will feel uncomfortable with the power of your silence and will probably begin to fill it in—often by backtracking and becoming more reasonable. You have nothing to lose by letting them do the talking at this point.

A variation of using silence is to walk away. "I'm willing to talk about this whenever you are willing to stop attacking me. Until then, we have nothing to talk about."

7. Sidestep/Ignore

Sidestepping or ignoring can be an effective response to personal attacks, extreme demands, and take-it-or-leave-it challenges. Instead of responding directly, act as if you didn't hear them. Change the topic and/or refocus the discussion on the underlying problem or conflict at hand.

Corporate Attorney: "I can't believe they pay you a professional salary."

Opposing Attorney: "I think we still have four issues we have not settled. Let's look at them one at a time."

Film Supplier: "The price is $10,000 per segment. Take it or leave it."

Production Manager: "Your tone of voice sounds angry. Do you feel as if we have not been fair to you in the past?"

or

"How many segments did you say you had?"

or

"What do you think would be fair criteria for deciding what the price should be?"

8. Don't Become Defensive Or Invite Criticism

Becoming defensive and justifying your position or needs encourages the other party to step up their attack. If you become defensive, they know that they have you on the run. Invite their criticism and refocus it as an attack on the problem needing to be solved. Invite them to explain how their comments will help solve the problem or conflict.

Magazine Editor: If you were committed to this magazine, you would have been here last week.

Art Director:

(Defensive Reply) I couldn't help it. I was burned out and needed the time off.

(Non-Defensive Reply) I know you are under a lot of pressure and last week was frustrating. What do you think we need to do so we don't get caught in that kind of last-minute bind in the future?

9. Refuse To Be Punished

Anyone has a right to be angry from time to time, but no one has the right to punish you. You do not deserve to be punished. You will know you are being punished when:

The other person keeps repeating their attack.

The other person vents their anger but refuses to tell you what they want from you behaviorally in response.

Refuse to be punished. Draw a boundary by asking the other person what they want from you. If their response is "I don't know," inform them that you are willing to continue the discussion when they do know. In the meantime, you're not willing to be punished.

10. Ask Questions

Making statements in which you take a stand will make the other person defensive. Instead, ask questions. Asking questions doesn't give them an object to attack and it invites them to justify their position or to vent their feelings. Asking questions gives you more information about the other party.

When asking your questions, ask "what" questions rather than "why" questions. "What" questions invite factual responses. "Why" questions are usually sneaky judgments that make the other party defensive. Listen to whether you want to make the other person feel guilty or whether you really want information. "What" questions will keep the negotiation moving. "Why" questions will tend to lead you to battle positions.

> (Attacking) Why did you think you could do that?
>
> (Information-seeking) What was your motivation for doing that?
>
> (Attacking) Why did you do that?
>
> (Information-seeking) What are the assumptions behind your actions?

11. Point Out Consequences

When the other person refuses to agree to a reasonable settlement, point out the consequences for them if you fail to reach an agreement. Try to present it as a statement of 'inevitable consequences' rather than as a threat.

"The reality is, if our company shows a loss again in the fourth quarter due to the strike, we will have no choice but to lay off five hundred union workers."

Summary

In this chapter we have seen some common Enforcer behavior patterns and a number of options for responding to them. Keep in mind the importance of getting the Enforcer's attention before anything else constructive is likely to happen. And remember, the bigger the bully, the more frightened the internal kid. Don't let yourself be bluffed by bullies. If they were really all that strong, they would be operating from a posture of quiet strength rather than trying to push you around.

CHAPTER 5

SCOREKEEPER PROFILE

Style of Thinking:	Concrete. Logical. Literal. Data-specific.
Way of Relating:	Utilitarian. Distrustful.
Core Needs:	A Fair Share.
Key Emotions:	Resentment. Feeling cheated or wary.
Sense of Power:	Being clever or descriptive. Positioning with people of influence.
Behavior:	Comparing. Keeping score. Seductive. Blaming. Withholding. Sulking. Deceiving. Being passive-aggressive, competitive, or manipulative.
Beliefs:	Someone owes me. Everyone's out to line his own pocket. Life's unfair. Never show all your cards. It's not my fault. I never get the breaks.
Style of Negotiating:	Strategizing. Bargaining. Convincing with logic. Dirty tricks. 50/50 compromise.

CHAPTER 5

SCOREKEEPERS: GETTING WHAT YOU WANT THROUGH MANIPULATION

As we have seen, adult Enforcers assume they have only two options for getting what they want from others. They either demand it, or they run away out of fear to hide.

Scorekeepers have more developed abilities for thinking and therefore have more options available to them to get what they want. In addition to demanding and withdrawing, they can also employ a wide assortment of manipulative strategies.

You are familiar with Scorekeepers. They are elementary schoolchildren walking around in adult bodies doing the best they know how to do to get what they need from others. Basically, they are afraid of not getting all that they need. They are afraid of being cheated or not getting their fair share. As a result, they keep trying to get more than enough through deceptive behavior.

For Scorekeepers, life is a plate of chocolate chip cookies and they have to grab theirs before someone beats them to it. So they keep score and plan their strategies to manipulate others. Scorekeepers are not very concerned whether others get what they need. They are primarily interested in making sure they get what they want for themselves. Scorekeepers' mottos are: "What is good for me is good for everyone"; "If it feels good, do it"; and "I've got to get my fair share."

How Do You Know When You Find One?

How do you know when you are dealing with a scorekeeper? Well, have you ever...

- Told your ten-year-old to vacuum the hallway and stairs and found he or she didn't think to vacuum the landing between?
- Told your housekeeper to organize the linens and afterwards found them in neat stacks, but you still didn't know where to find the king-sized sheets or the double sheets, the flat or fitted sheets?
- Been frustrated when an employee didn't do the job you wanted done and mumbled under your breath, "Why doesn't he think for himself?"
- Been in an argument with someone who took everything you said literally and missed the real meaning of your message?
- Felt as if you always have to do more than your share?
- Counted how many packages there were for you under the Christmas tree?
- Made a mental note that you spent more on someone's gift than they spent on yours?
- Confronted an employee about his or her performance and had him or her respond that it was unfair because you hadn't confronted other employees about the same behavior?
- Felt like someone was trying to cheat or deceive you?
- Felt someone was being nice to you because they wanted something from you?
- Tried to figure out a sneaky way to pay someone back?
- Used logic to attempt to convince someone that you were right and they were wrong?
- Pretended to not understand?
- Lied to get what you wanted from someone?

- Planned how to take advantage of another person?
- Pouted, sulked, forgot, became sick, or tried some other passive-aggressive behavior to get what you want?
- Complained that life isn't fair because others get more than you do?
- Felt resentful when someone cut in front of you?
- Known someone who always had an excuse for his behavior, pointed the finger elsewhere, loved to get into a Blame Game?

If you answered "yes" to any of these, you were either dealing with a Scorekeeper or you were one.

Scorekeeper Scenarios

The following scenarios give you some examples of Scorekeeper situations:

Imagine union and management negotiating teams sitting down across the table from each other. Members are cordial to one another, but behind their smiles they are sizing up the other side. Members of the management team know there is some dissension within the opposition and are wondering how they can use it as a wedge to divide and conquer the union. Members of the union team feel they made too many concessions the last time around because of the depressed economy. They are determined to reestablish the union's power and authority in the organization.

Imagine yourself going to buy a new car. You don't know much about buying cars and feel a little intimidated. You certainly don't trust car salesmen. You're wondering what kind of trick the salesperson will try to play on you. You don't trust his overly friendly manner.

Imagine yourself as an account executive for an advertising firm. Your client wants you to lower costs in the proposal and to commit to having the campaign ready in four weeks. You could do both and still make a reasonable profit, but you figure that if you hold out, she'll come around.

Imagine yourself in a courtroom watching a defense attorney barrage a witness with questions, hoping to confuse him so he will contradict himself.

Imagine yourself as a supervisor confronting an employee about consistently coming to work late. You assume that the employee resents the performance review you gave him and is passively aggressively paying you back by showing up late. The employee denies this and says it is not his fault that he is late.

These scenarios all have something in common. In all of them, people don't trust each other. They assume they have to watch out and be more clever than the other party. What causes Scorekeepers to be manipulative to get what they need? Why do they believe they must strategize and be sneaky and bargain? Why do they compare what they have with what others have? The answer lies in their level of thinking.

Scorekeeper Literal Thinking

Unlike Enforcers, Scorekeepers can think rationally. They have the ability to be logical and sequential, but under one condition—they need concrete, specific, sensory data. They need to have all the pieces laid out in front of them. Then they can plan a sequence of steps to solve a problem or complete a task. They can think logically if the objects or persons are concretely present or visible. Their logic is a logic of objects, not theories about objects. They do not have the capacity for abstract thinking. They think and hear literally.

Once, when my boys were young, I told them to clean the garage and busied myself doing something else. When I went out later to check on them, they weren't doing the job. In my estimation, they were messing around. But in reality, they didn't have the ability to figure out how to do the job. They needed concrete, specific instructions.

I told the boys there were four categories of items in the garage—bicycle parts, lawn equipment, sporting equipment, and cleaning supplies. I wanted them to move everything out of the garage and sweep it. Then I told them where to put each group of items. Once I had given them the categories and the steps in the process, they could do the job.

It wasn't long after this that my oldest son, Andy, developed the ability to think abstractly, the next stage of thinking. I would tell the boys to go clean the garage, and Andy would have the whole project figured out in his head on the way out the door. He would then assign the jobs to the other boys and take off on his bicycle. There are advantages to developing higher levels of thinking!

We encounter this same type of literal thinking in business when we give an employee an assignment and then find out it wasn't completed the way we needed it done. The reality is, Scorekeepers are not good at reading minds and filling in the blanks.

As these examples point out, Scorekeepers tend to be literal in their thinking. They literally interpret rules and beliefs and instructions. They will literally hold you to what you say instead of hearing the meaning of your message.

An example is the sales manager who tries to hold you to the sales bonus you promised but fails to consider the other important criteria for the bonus—the company's percentage of profit. The facts that the market was depressed and that the sales team poorly managed their overhead are forgotten.

In a negotiation, Scorekeepers will expect the other side to prove their facts and figures. They will more likely be convinced through concrete, logical arguments than through emotional persuasion.

This was true in a negotiation with South American shippers. The purpose of the meeting was to reach agreement on the adjustments due for damaged goods. The shippers' style of negotiation was highly emotional uproar. They assumed they could squeeze more concessions from my client by responding dramatically. Every item on the adjustment list was a personal affront. In turn, they had a long list of grievances and attempted to get the members of our negotiating team to point the finger at each other. The only effective response to their melodrama was to continually ask them for their factual data and to present them with our financial and dock inspection data. Fortunately, my client had his claims well substantiated.

Unlike Enforcers, Scorekeepers accurately understand the perspective of another person if that perspective is concretely related to their own experience and interest. In this we see the beginnings of a capacity for empathy. However, Scorekeepers will not understand the perspective of people they perceive to be different from them. Thus, in the sessions with our South American shippers, I was careful to preface my claims with "We both know what it is like to deal with. . . ."

The sales staff will understand each other's perspectives and needs, but may have a more difficult time understanding the views of the production department. The union members all make sense to one another, but they don't understand management's thinking.

Scorekeepers may not have much empathy for understanding others who are different from them. They have learned to be more disciplined and to hide their feelings when it suits their purpose. If they are angry, they will look for sneaky or passive-aggressive ways to let you know. They know how to be deceptive and lie. They know the value of a poker face. They know how to be resentful.

Common emotions for Scorekeepers include:

Resentment
Feeling cheated
Feeling neglected
Feeling cautious
Feeling wary
Feeling deceptive
Feeling distrustful
Feeling competitive
Fear of missing something
Feeling like they're not enough
Feeling coy or seductive
Fear of not getting a fair share
Feeling taken advantage of
Fear of not measuring up

How Scorekeepers Do It

Given their literal style of thinking and their fear of not getting enough, Scorekeepers employ a spectrum of passive and active manipulative behaviors to get what they want. Their approach to negotiating is to strategize, play games, bargain, and compromise. Scorekeeper behavior is common in political life and in the business community. In fact, a high percentage of business transactions are probably carried out on Scorekeeper levels. Favorite behaviors of Scorekeepers include:

Planning strategies
Being clever
Being coy
Acting confused
Being persuasive
Being a sneaky rebel
Being dramatic
Being martyred
Playing helpless
Being charming
Bargaining
Withholding
Being grabby
Having hidden agendas
Self-sabotaging
Coming late
Excusing oneself
Being "on-guard"
Playing "Poor me"
Sighing
Withholding information
Trading favors
Throwing temper tantrums
Working hard, then slacking off
Wearing the other person down with pleading
Comparing self to others
Waiting and keeping score
Being sexually seductive
Playing dumb
Denying
Lying
Playing "uproar"
Pitting people against each other
Testing to see how much can be obtained
Blaming
Playing touché
Convincing with logic
Being passively resistant
Being passively aggressive
Getting sick
Pouting
Pretending
Doing favors
Using silent treatment
"Fair trade" 50/50 compromising

"YOU SCRATCH MY BACK AND I'LL SCRATCH YOURS"

Scorekeepers view everyone else in relation to themselves. They do not view others as having value separate from themselves. Scorekeeper relationships are based on mutual exchange or reciprocity. For them, relationships are utilitarian. Others are important only in terms of what they can provide the Scorekeeper or prevent the Scorekeeper from getting.

Using the example of the South American shippers again, no real trust or loyalty or mutual commitment existed between them and my client. My client was only important to them because they had not found a more profitable deal. The deal itself was only as good as last season's performance.

Scorekeepers realize that others have needs and interests that are different from theirs, and they assume that others are like them in wanting to get all they can. In order to get what they want from others, Scorekeepers will use deception to trick others into cooperating. If their deceptive behavior doesn't work, they are prepared to reciprocate with some item or service of equal value.

Another Scorekeeper motto is "I'll con you if I can get away with it. If that doesn't work, I'll do you a favor if you'll do me a favor." So, if their strategies do not work in a negotiation, they will resort to bargaining and compromise, provided it is a fair 50/50 compromise. They'll take 100 percent if they can get it, but they won't settle for 49 percent.

The South American shippers never expected to get the outrageous claims they were requesting. But to their way of thinking, they had to begin with outrageous claims in order to have bargaining chips later on.

The morality of a Scorekeeper is based on the assumption that everyone is out to line his or her own pocket. They are not particularly concerned whether others get what they need. The South Americans wanted everything they could get out of the deal and assumed the same was true for my client. Because they are more aware and therefore more effective, Scorekeepers are even more self-interested than Enforcers. It is a common stance among people in business.

As a result, Scorekeepers have a heightened sense of justice or paranoia. Scorekeepers are constantly afraid of being cheated and not getting their fair share. They keep count. They are always watching their left flank to make sure someone doesn't take advantage of them.

Anyone with elementary schoolchildren has endured their constant scorekeeping:

"It's my turn to go first."

"If he gets three, I get three."

"She got to sit by the window on the way to the store."

I learned years ago that there are not enough windows in a station wagon for even two kids to feel they have been treated fairly.

We often operate the same way in our adult relationships. Have you ever said to yourself, "How come I'm the only one who ever

. . . takes out the garbage?

. . . fills the ice cube trays?

. . . puts a new roll of toilet paper in the holder?

. . . initiates the lovemaking?

. . . has to get up with the kids?

. . . plans our social activities?

. . . has to work so hard?"

If so, you know that your loving relationship has just degenerated into a scorekeeping business affair.

We see the same type of resentment and paranoia in business. Scorekeepers add up their offenses and use the resentment to justify deceptive business practices. I recall a financial consultant who told me he was going to resign from his company because his boss had not kept his promises. As I listened to his list of examples, I wondered why he had tolerated such abuse for so long.

Two weeks later, I found out. I discovered there was another side to all of his complaints. I also discovered he had attempted to go behind his boss' back and steal several key customers to set up his own business. Scorekeepers are good at deceiving themselves to justify their deceptive behavior.

What Scorekeepers Are Saying To Themselves

Some of the common beliefs underlying Scorekeeper relationships are:

- Somebody owes me.
- How come I'm the one who always has to. . . ?
- Life is unfair.
- I didn't get my share.
- It's my turn.
- Everyone is out for his own advantage.
- Screw them before they screw you.
- It's not safe to be transparent.
- Charity begins at home.
- I don't get angry, I just get even.
- It wasn't my fault.
- You can get more by being clever than by being honest.
- If I do them a favor, then they'll owe me one.

Scorekeeper Power

For Scorekeepers, power resides in aligning themselves with influential people. In other words, if you can give me what I want, you're important to me. I'll be very nice to you and take you to lunch, if I need a business favor from you, or if I need to win you over to my side in a dispute.

The Scorekeeper's power in a negotiation also lies in being clever and knowing better strategies than his opponent. When he attends a seminar on negotiating, the Scorekeeper is primarily interested in learning specific strategies and more effective dirty tricks so as not to "leave any more money than necessary on the table."

Since he believes everyone is out for himself, he has to be smarter than the next guy in order to get his share of the cookies. In business, it's called "gaining the competitive edge in a tight market." Similarly, Scorekeepers tend to distrust persons in authority since they assume authority figures are using their position to line their own pockets.

Implications For Negotiating From A Scorekeeper Stance

The implications for negotiating from a Scorekeeper stance carry with them good news (in comparison with Enforcers that is) and bad news. The good news is that because of their increased capacities, Scorekeepers have more behavioral options in a negotiating situation. And if they are good strategizers, they can be financially successful.

The bad news is that their options are still pretty limited and in the long run are not very effective. Scorekeepers can win skirmishes, but they don't have much chance of achieving a peaceful treaty. They can do a better job of solving problems than can Enforcers, but they are dismal at building productive ongoing relationships because they do not trust anyone and no one trusts them. Under these circumstances, it is hard to build long-term, satisfying relationships.

But the worst irony for Scorekeepers is that while they can accumulate a lot of wealth, they cannot rest and enjoy it. They always have to be watching their left flank, afraid that someone may try to even the score. The more they acquire, the more they 'have' to defend. They become more paranoid and their possessions end up owning them. Some specific implications:

1. As a Scorekeeper, you will be able to think in a consistently logical, orderly manner. You will be able to plan for your negotiations: to gather specific data and to analyze the problem. You will have some idea of causes, and you will be able to stay "on track" more often than an Enforcer will. However, your thinking will tend to be limited to planning better strategies so you don't leave as much on the table the next time.

2. You will be more disciplined than an Enforcer and better able to control your emotions. Your behavior will be more appropriate, and you will be less obvious in your self-protectiveness. Instead of blowing up when you're angry, you'll be logical and try to convince the other person that he or she is wrong—or you'll give them the silent treatment. You'll know the value of a poker face. You'll know how to withhold data that might be used against you.

3. You will be literal in your thinking. In your literalness, you will sometimes misinterpret the meaning of others' behavior and miss the main point they are trying to make. The other party's silence does not always mean they are planning strat-

egies against you. Their rescheduling of a meeting does not necessarily mean they are stalling.

4. You will not be able to understand underlying principles and values if they are abstract. 'Fairness' to a Scorekeeper means they get three if you got three. You may not understand the relative value or long-term value of a contract term.

5. You will be unable to step back from your experience and reflect on it. You will not be able to adopt a third-person perspective, to be aware of another process going on at the same time you are negotiating. Thus you may fail to appreciate that both of you are simply pointing the finger at each other. You may fail to appreciate that as long as both of you wait for the other party to admit it was all his fault, you may wait for a long, long time.

6. You will be so busy planning your defense that you will not be able to accurately listen to the other person. As a result, you will tend to inaccurately perceive his needs and the obvious solutions that would meet both of your needs.

An example:

Caesar and Mike are partners in a trucking company. Caesar is the creative, entrepreneurial risk-taker type who doesn't want to be restrained. As a result, he has repeatedly pushed the company to its financial brink by making unplanned acquisitions and capital expenditures. His pattern is to act and let others know later.

Mike, the company's financial officer, is more methodical and wants more controlled growth for the business. Resentment and distrust have built up between them because of Caesar's pattern of buy now, tell later.

Their conflict erupted again over whether to buy twenty new flatbed trucks to accommodate the special needs of a new customer. Each of them was so busy justifying his own position that they failed to see an obvious solution—to modify some of their refrigerated trucks, which were not being used, with new support frames. Luckily, their chief mechanic was able to intercede with the solution before they lost the customer.

7. You will tend to be paranoid, to falsely assume that everyone is always out after his own gain. As a result, you will set

up others to be competitive with you and to mistrust you. You'll invite them to be deceptive with you, to use all their dirty tricks. Potential allies will become antagonists.

Some Examples:

Alice, a payroll clerk, was certain her new supervisor wanted to get rid of her. As a result, Alice denied responsibility for mistakes she made and tried to shift the blame to others. These behaviors caused her new supervisor to distrust her and to put her on probation.

Sam was certain that another salesman wanted his accounts and was trying to make Sam look bad to their sales manager. So Sam began withholding information and making derogatory comments about the other salesman. As word leaked back about Sam's behavior, the other salesman began retaliating. The competitive conflict between them became so intense, the sales manager decided one of them had to go. Sam was fired. He had created what he feared most.

8. You will limit yourself to game-playing or to solutions in which neither party gets what they really want. You will be unable to create novel, innovative solutions.

9. Instead of understanding negotiating as a mutual search for solutions, you will see it as competitive one-upmanship in which you are maneuvering to outwit your opponent. Your primary motivation will be to avoid being cheated or taken advantage of instead of solving problems to both party's mutual satisfaction. And you will falsely assume that your greatest power lies in being more clever.

Operating from a Scorekeeper stance is the traditional approach to negotiating. When people talk about negotiating, they are usually thinking in terms of strategizing, game-playing, bargaining, and compromising. The commonly-used term for formal union negotiating—collective bargaining—reflects this attitude. However, the limitations of Scorekeeping far outweigh its advantages. Scorekeepers do not stand up well against skillful No-Fault Negotiators.

How do you successfully negotiate with a Scorekeeper? Options detailed in the next chapter give you the information you need.

CHAPTER 6

BEATING SCOREKEEPERS AT THEIR OWN GAMES

Scorekeepers come in a wide variety of colors, shapes, and sizes. What they all have in common are deception and keeping score to make sure they aren't cheated. They are out for their own best advantage and they assume everyone else is too. They plan their strategies, use any form of manipulation that will work, and are actively or passively aggressive. When all else fails, they bargain and compromise (provided they can achieve a fair trade, 50/50 compromise).

Basically, Scorekeepers do what they do because they don't trust. They don't trust that others will treat them fairly. They don't trust that others will want to cooperate with them. They don't trust that others will give them what they want if they ask for it in straight ways. They believe they have to be deceptive.

Your primary strategy for negotiating with Scorekeepers is to negotiate the process (the rules of the game—how you are going to negotiate with each other) and the criteria (what the fair standards for settlement will be) before talking about the specific content.

This is important for two reasons. The first is that you want to lock them into fair processes and standards before you begin so they don't change the rules and the finish line on you during the negotiation. The second reason is that by establishing the process and criteria up front, they know what the rules are going to be. They know what to expect. This helps them to be more trusting and less likely to feel the need to be deceptive.

For example:

Car dealers frequently play the game of "wear them down." They always want you to make a written offer first, and only then do you find out that the salesperson does not have the authority to accept the offer. The salesperson disappears into the sales manager's office and eventually comes back and informs you that the sales manager (the bad guy) won't accept the offer. After several rounds of this, as the customer becomes weary, they bring in a fresh recruit to continue the process until they have gotten all they can out of you.

Next time you want to buy a car, negotiate the process and criteria for settlement up front. (And go on Sunday evening about 8:30 because the sales manager probably will not be there and the salesperson, if it has been a non-productive weekend, will be more motivated to sell.)

First Negotiate The Process

Before looking at a car, tell the salesperson you will buy a car from him provided two conditions are met: first, you find a car you like; second, the salesperson will bring out the computer sheet (or index card) that shows exactly how much they have invested in the car you like (or, you can call a financial institution and find out the dealer cost beforehand and do this over the phone). It is only fair that you both have the same information base.

Then Negotiate The Criteria

Once you have seen the information, offer to pay them $200 over their cost.

If the salesperson doesn't agree to your process and criteria, move on down the road. You'll find plenty who will.

Other examples of negotiating the process and criteria up front with a Scorekeeper:

- If your boss habitually forgets what you both agreed about a raise, put the agreement (amount of raise, when it's applicable, and performance criteria) in writing and have both of you sign off on it.
- If the union bargaining committee refuses to make decisions and seems to resist cooperating, find out what the reasons are, or what prevents them from reaching cooperative decisions, or what it would cost them if they did. Find a way to remove the blocks in the process.

In this case, when senior managers finally did the obvious thing and asked, they were surprised to find that the union committee didn't make decisions because they were never notified of meetings beforehand, were always surprised by the agenda, and were not permitted to meet during work hours to discuss issues. Senior management always controlled or led the meetings and when the union wasn't immediately agreeable, management accused them of not being cooperative. The union resented management's behavior and intentionally delayed decisions.

Cooperation increased, and decisions began to be made more quickly when the management team showed the union committee an agenda in advance and provided them time to meet beforehand to discuss issues. Through discussions between the corporate president and the chairman of the union committee, agreement was reached that the contract did not always have to be literally followed if they reached mutual agreement on the need to make exceptions, which was a change in both process and criteria.

How to negotiate process and criteria up front is described in detail in Chapter 13 on Shift Your Focus.

There are many different types of Scorekeepers, and their strategies are usually subtle. I will list specific responses as I describe each type. The responses vary in confrontational strength. The general rule of thumb is to begin with more gentle confrontations. When you don't get the other person's attention with the gentle confrontation, then you need to become more firm and more direct.

SCOREKEEPER TYPES: DECEIVERS, PEONS, FOGGERS, DUMMIES, ESCALATORS, POUTERS, JAILERS, ETC.

1. **Deceivers.** Deceivers lie. They:

a. Make promises they do not intend to keep, or they try to convince you to trust them so they can take advantage of you.

"I'll do whatever you want."

"I promise to be there."

"I'll have it done by Tuesday."

"I will be honest with you..."

"I'd like to help."

b. Lead you to believe they have more authority or competence than they have.

"I can do the job for you."

"Make me an offer...and then I'll tell you that I have to take it to my sales manager."

"I'm just the person you need."

"I know everything there is to know about..."

c. Make claims about their products that are not true.

"Our software is the best on the market."

"This car was owned by a little old lady from..."

"You won't find a better buy."

"It gets thirty miles per gallon in town."

d. Excuse themselves from wrongdoing.

"I didn't do it."

"I wasn't there."

"John was the last one to use the..."

"I told you the truth."

e. Lie about their costs or are deceptive about the total cost you'll have to pay.

"I have to send this out to have it done. My overhead is so high I can't do it any cheaper."

"Now, there is a minor service charge I forgot to mention."

f. Misrepresent the facts.

"Our statistics show that..."

"I was here at five o'clock."

"He started it."

"I tried to call you several times."

g. Change the rules and suddenly you find that old rules have been modified or new rules have been added.

"I forgot to mention that the eight of hearts is wild." (I just happen to have it in my hand.)

"Now that you have signed your offer, I'll have to take it to my sales manager for approval."

"Oh, by the way, the deposit has to be paid before I can confirm your reservation."

"Matt won't be back until next Friday. We won't be able to get this signed until then."

In Response:

Confront them directly. Confront their intentions, authority, and behavior. Ask them to verify their promises and facts and insist on fair criteria and procedures. If you are contracting for a product or service, send a purchase order and mark on it "Total cost." If they act offended, say that you trust them. Make it clear that you just want to be fair and not have any misunderstandings later on.

"I assume you are telling me the truth and therefore assume you won't mind explaining... I need to understand how you arrived at your figures."

"I was under the impression that you had the authority to approve my offer. I'd like to speak directly to your sales manager."

"I'm not willing to change the rules in the middle of the game. You did not mention that rule before we began."

"I know that the bluebook value of my car is $400 more than your quote. I suggest we bring in an independent appraiser."

"What guarantee do I have that it will be done Tuesday? What will the consequences be if it isn't?"

2. **Peons.** Peons pretend they are nobody or not important. They put themselves down before somebody else does. That way, no one can hold them responsible or have expectations of them.

"I'm just a dumb farmer."

"You're asking the wrong person."

"I just run the errands around here."

"What do I know?"

In Response:

Don't let them get away with it.

"You look smart enough to me."

"If you don't know, who does?"

"Well, if you run all the errands around here, then you must know what's going on."

"My guess is you know enough."

3. **Foggers**. Foggers are masters of confusion. As long as they can keep you confused, you can't nail them down or get to the real issues. They will talk excessively, ramble, go in circles, and bring in every irrelevant detail they can muster. (Examples would just be confusing.)

In Response:

Shut them up, interrupt them, point out that you are getting confused, summarize what you are hearing, refocus on the real issues (if you can find them), ask them to tell you briefly what you want to know from them, or ask them to help you clarify where you both are.

"Let me interrupt you for a minute."

"What I hear you saying is . . . I'm not sure what that has to do with the problem."

"Let's try to boil this down and focus on the primary concerns."

"Tell me in two sentences what you just said."

4. **Dummies**. Dummies are behaviorally similar to Withdrawers. The difference is that Dummies play dumb as a strategy rather than out of fear.

"I didn't know they had already made the decision."

"Beats me."

"I dunno."

"I can't remember."

"Nobody told me about it."

"I didn't know that when I talked to . . ."

In Response:

Don't buy it.

"If you did know, what would you say?"

"Guess."

"I don't understand what 'I don't know' means."

"Exactly what is it that you don't know?"

5. **Escalators**. Escalators keep taking one more bite. Just when you think you've got an agreement, they add another demand or they go back and open up an issue that you thought was already settled.

"There's one more issue that we need to address."

"I want to talk about the procedure for appraising the contract again."

"I'm not clear what we decided about who would pay for the installation."

In Response:

Confront the issue directly.

"We've already decided that."

"We have an agreement and I expect you to honor it."

"You keep adding more conditions. I think you are trying to see how much you can get out of us. I don't like that."

6. **Pouters**. Pouting is one of the passive-aggressive forms of manipulation. Pouters will sulk and punish by giving you the silent treatment. In turn, you are supposed to feel guilty and bad. They don't say anything, but this is what they are silently thinking.

"I won't call (write to) them and they'll call me."

"If I hold out long enough, they'll give in."

"I won't talk to them and then they'll feel bad."

In Response:

Name the game and make it clear that you refuse to be punished or to feel guilty. If the Pouter wants a response from you, they'll have to find a more effective way to get it. In the meantime, go about your own affairs and ignore them. If you give in, know that you have just invited them to do it again. When they no longer get a payoff, they'll stop pouting.

"Let me know when you want to talk. In the meantime, I have other things to do."

"You need to understand that pouting doesn't work with me. I don't accept silent punishment."

"You can be miserable as long as you want and that still isn't going to get you what you want from me."

7. **Jailers**. Jailers attempt to lock you in by making public statements to embarrass you, by getting you to agree to conditions that will put you at a disadvantage later on, or by trying to make you honor old agreements that are no longer valid.

"The management team has refused to negotiate in good faith."

"The union bargainers stated that they would..."

"We will meet only if the attorneys are not present."

"You promised!"

In Response:

If you suspect that the other party will try to lock you in by making public statements to embarrass you, one option is to negotiate an agreement beforehand about what will be said in public. It is often a good idea to get this in writing and have the document signed. This is also a situation in which you can sometimes point out the consequences for the other party if they choose to use this tactic.

Don't allow yourself to be railroaded. Consider the consequences before agreeing to conditions. Take a break. Tell them you need time to think about it or discuss it. Stall.

When someone tries to hold you to an agreement that is no longer valid, acknowledge the old agreement. Say that conditions have changed and explain why you can no longer honor the old agreement. Draw your boundary.

> "I am willing to publicly announce that you have decided to resign in order to take a sabbatical to go back to school. I will not make any public or private statements that I fired you, provided you are willing to do the same. If you attempt to create a public issue out of this, I will be forced to present my documentation to the entire Board. I will not have any other choice. Are you willing to agree to this and to sign a mutual press release?"

> "We have not had an opportunity to consider your proposal. We will need to meet alone to discuss it before I can give you an answer."

> "It's true that I recommended that you get a 5 percent raise. However, that was before the salary freeze was put into effect by top management. I understand your frustration, but I cannot do anything about the freeze."

> "I agreed to let you use the car before I found out you were failing all of your classes. I am not willing to reward you for flunking out of school and I want you to know how serious I am about you bringing your grades up."

8. **Stern, Silent Partners**. The Silent Partner game is a maneuver to get you to make greater concessions. Using this tactic, the

other person tells you he would like to be able to agree to your request or offer, but his supervisor (wife, friend, boss, sales manager) would never agree to it. His hands are tied.

"If it were up to me, I'd say go ahead, but my partner will never go for it."

"If I took that offer to my client, he'd laugh me out of the room."

"I'm afraid my wife would hit the ceiling if I agreed to that."

In Response:

Attempt to focus on the underlying issues by asking questions. Ask the other person to explain specifically what he anticipates his partner's concerns to be. This will clarify for you his hidden position. Then ask him to verify his position by asking what he thinks is the basis for his partner's concerns. If this doesn't get results, ask to speak directly to the partner. If neither strategy works, suggest a tentative agreement that you both will go home and consider the issues and concerns.

"Can you explain to me specifically what you think your partner's response will be? What do you think his concerns are? Why do you think he would take that position? What would he need to be willing to agree to this?"

"How would it be if I talked directly to your wife?"

"I'd like to suggest that we both consider this a tentative agreement. You take it back to your client and discuss it, and I'll think some more about it myself. We can meet on Monday and see where we are then."

9. **Uproar Inventors**. Uproar Inventors are stage directors. They stir everything up so the opposition will kill off each other. Their basic strategy is to hook everyone into Enforcer behavior, get them fighting with each other, and then step back and watch. Their intention is to shift the attention away from themselves.

This game commonly occurs in families. The parent gets home from a bad day at work and immediately begins blasting everyone out of the water. "Whose bike is that in the driveway?

Whose socks are on the table? Who made that mess in the family room? How come the yard isn't finished? You damn kids just lie around here all day looking for messes to make." In under sixty seconds, all the kids will be fighting with each other over who made what mess and everyone will be excusing himself from responsibility.

Another family variation is one in which the parent and child argue over what the kid will wear to church or to visit the grandparents. The kid has learned to neither agree nor disagree. He simply disappears until everyone is getting into the car. As he walks out in his unacceptable attire, he can get his parents fighting with each other over how each of them handled the situation and why they are late. From here they can quickly degenerate into sharing their opinions about each other's mother.

This strategy is also common in business. The Uproar Inventor will use shock, attacks, snipes, insinuations, dramatic accusations, and gossip. His hidden purpose is either to get everyone fighting with each other or to so hook his opposition into Enforcer behavior that he loses his power and his capacity to think and behave rationally.

> "The information that I have received indicates malpractice. I think we have grounds for litigation."
>
> "I think he was drinking."
>
> "I would have thought that a man in your position would have handled that better."
>
> "If you knew what went on when you were gone . . . well, I'm not going to say anything."
>
> "I think you're naive about what people are really saying behind your back."
>
> "Herb told me that he didn't trust you and that he would never recommend your proposals to the committee." (At this point, you probably don't trust anyone, and you are also faced with the dilemma of whether or not to confront Herb.)
>
> "I talked to your ex-partner over lunch. He had some interesting comments to make that I'm not free to

pass on."

"If your team hadn't bungled the job in the beginning, we wouldn't be in this mess now."

In Response:

Resist becoming defensive. Rather than join their game, calmly acknowledge that there may be some truth to their accusations and ask them to verify their facts. Refuse to play. Let them know that you have no intention of getting caught in the middle and that you don't accept third-party information.

Confront them by describing their behavior and ask them what their motivation is. Let them know you are not willing to be sidetracked from the real issues between you. By doing this, you will be refocusing the negotiation. Call them on their belief by suggesting you all sit down together.

Uproar Inventor:

"I don't know why you're talking to me. You oughta be talking to that sleazy partner of yours. You better wake up and find out what he was doing when you were gone."

Response:

"Perhaps I should—but I'm not sure what that has to do with you not living up to your contract. If you can tell me what was going on and how that prevented you from doing what you agreed to do, I'm willing to listen."

Uproar Inventor:

"I think you better ask Al yourself. You're too dumb to know when you're getting taken."

Response:

"That may be true. What I am aware of right now is that you are not giving me concrete answers as to why you failed to complete the work. Instead, you are making insinuations, calling me names, and suggesting I shouldn't trust Al. I think you're trying to take the heat off yourself. If I'm being naive about Al, I'm the one who will pay the price. But that is a separate issue from what we are addressing now. I make it a point to not accept third-party accusations that are not backed up by specific data. And I am not willing to be sidetracked from the real issue here."

Uproar Inventor:

"Nobody can work with him."

Response:

"I'm hearing that you and Al have some problems to work out. I'm not willing to get caught between the two of you."

Uproar Inventor:

"It's not just me. You don't know what's been going on. And you don't know what Stu said about you."

Response:

"Well, if Stu has something to say to me, he can say it to me directly. Once again you are making vague accusations. If you can substantiate your accusations now and convince me, I'm willing to sit down with the two of you and confront whatever is going on. If you're not willing to substantiate your allegations and if you're not willing to sit down face to face, then I can only assume that you are trying to pit Al and me against each other so you can sidestep your responsibility. I intend to hold you to your contract, unless there is a valid reason why you couldn't do the work."

Uproar Inventor:

"I'm not the only one who didn't finish his work."

Response:

"We're not talking about anyone else right now. We're talking about you."

10. **Active Waiters**. Waiters wait. They wait because they hope that maybe the problem will go away in time, or the conflict will blow over and be forgotten. They wait because it may be to their advantage to stall. If they stall long enough, you may not be able

to do anything about the situation because the deadline has passed.

The kid knows that if he puts off cleaning up the kitchen long enough, you'll have to do it yourself before you fix dinner. The union negotiator knows that he will have more leverage once the contract has run out and the union has the freedom to call for a strike vote. The parent hopes that if he puts off the request to buy a dog, the kid may forget about it.

You may want to prevent a developer from building condominiums next to your property. Your efforts in negotiating with the developer and your appeal to the zoning board have been unsuccessful, so you approach a city official and ask him to intercede. The city official doesn't want to be associated with the problem. He wants to avoid public criticism that might arise if he takes a stand on either side, so he stalls. He knows that once the foundations are poured, he can say he tried but it was too late. You can usually tell when you are encountering a Waiter when the other party makes excuses to explain why he can't meet or is not available, when he is ambiguous, avoids making a commitment, or avoids coming to a resolution.

"I'll do it later."

"I want to think about it."

"I'll try to see what I can do."

"I'm not sure how soon I can get to it."

"I'll do the best I can."

"I'll get back to you."

"Call my secretary about an appointment. I don't have my book with me."

11. **Passive-aggressive Waiters**. The Passive-aggressive Waiter feels cheated or mistreated and is waiting for someone to recognize that fact. He is waiting for his "just rewards." Somebody owes him something and they should want to give it to him. So he waits. And while he waits, he keeps adding up the tally and counting his grievances. Someday, when he has enough, he'll cash them in and try to make somebody pay. Maybe.

Passive-aggressive Waiters can be very difficult to deal with. You do not always know they are waiting or why they are waiting. Often you only know after the fact that you have a Passive-aggressive Waiter to contend with. Eventually they will let you know that you have been insensitive or unfair and that they have been cheated. This is often done with ambiguous or glancing comments designed to make you feel obligated and guilty. You, in turn, are supposed to guess what you did wrong.

"You could have called."

"I thought you would be home earlier."

"I never get any recognition around here."

"You seemed to have plenty of time over the past month to have lunch with other people."

"You've never supported me."

In Response:

One option is to establish deadlines. Try to get the other party to commit to a specific time when you will receive an answer or when a decision will be made. A second option is to name the game openly. Games lose much of their power when they are no longer a secret maneuver. A third option is to point out the consequences for the other side if they wait. Again, this should be stated as a substantiated warning of what will unavoidably happen rather than as a threat.

"I'd be more comfortable if we could set a specific time when you will get back to me with an answer. That way I will be able to better plan what I need to do."

"I feel like I'm being put off. If that is not your intention, then I assume you are willing to make a commitment now."

"We are all aware that it is to your advantage to not arrive at a resolution until after the contract runs out. It seems to me that you are stalling until you have more leverage."

"If we have not reached substantive agreements by the fifteenth, then our company will begin preparations for a lockout if you decide to strike. We can continue to operate

> the plant indefinitely with our non-union personnel. In fact, that will save us considerable overhead costs. Your members will be the losers."

A fourth option is a stronger variation of all those above—confront them. Let them know you are not willing to be put off. Getting their attention in this manner can be effective if you have any leverage to back up the boundary you have drawn.

> "I'm not willing to be put off again. I want to know specifically what you intend to do."

> "I assume that you probably wish this whole situation would just go away. You probably don't want to get caught in the middle. At the same time, it is important to me to come to some resolution. I am not willing to be put off or to wait passively until it is too late for negotiation. If I do not hear from you by next Wednesday, then I will be forced to go to the newspapers."

A fifth option that applies primarily to Passive-aggressive Waiters is to let them know that you are a miserable mind reader.

> "If you don't tell me specifically what it is that you want, don't expect me to guess."

> "It feels as if you've been silently waiting and tallying up your grievances with me. I'm not willing to be responsible for guessing what you want."

12. **Blamers**. Blamers blame—both actively and passively. The intention of Blamers is to shift the responsibility away from themselves. They want to be right; they want someone else to take the rap (or they want someone else to be responsible for them); they want to punish someone else in sneaky ways so it won't come back on them.

Active Blamers have multiple strategies. They are fond of using logic to convince you that you are wrong and they are right. They will use rhetorical questions or "why" questions in an attempt to back you into a corner so you can hang yourself. These statements and questions are accompanied by an accusing tone of voice.

"If you didn't have anything to hide, you would have called me yesterday."

"Do you think everyone should be allowed to come to work whenever they feel like it?"

"Why didn't you let me know that all the orders were not completed?"

"How do you think that makes the rest of us feel?"

Active Blamers are greasy. They are masters at slipping out of any responsibility. It is never their fault. Somebody else did it. They always have a ready excuse.

"Don't talk to me about it. I wasn't even there when it happened."

"I wasn't the last one to use it."

"Nobody told me not to use it."

"He did it, not me."

Active Blamers have elephant memories. They never forget or forgive a past offense. They keep dragging up the past to beat you in the present. They literally hold you to what you said.

"You didn't get your part finished last week."

"I told you not to throw it away."

"Well, you always do that to me."

Active Blamers want to make someone else pay. They want someone else to be responsible for their lives.

"They wouldn't let me."

"It's their fault that I couldn't. . ."

"If you hadn't been so careless we wouldn't have this problem now."

Passive Blamers are sometimes more subtle. They like to snipe, to give unasked for, 'helpful' feedback to tell you what others are saying, and to let you know how you have disappointed them—again.

"You're so busy these days you obviously don't have time for your friends."

"Your magazine is great. I did notice a few glaring mistakes that a magazine of this quality shouldn't have. Let me show them to you."

"You were never there when I needed you."

In Response:

Once again, name the game to defuse its power and to refocus on the issues.

"Your words and tone of voice sound blaming. We could waste time trading accusations back and forth, but I don't see that as helping us get to a resolution. I suggest we address the real issues."

Decline to be blamed or to take responsibility for the other party. Make the other party take responsibility by asking him to translate his blaming statements and questions into specific requests.

"What I hear in your rhetorical questions are really blaming statements. Tell me directly what it is you want from me."

"I am not willing to be blamed or to take responsibility for you. I'd like to hear specifically what it is that you need and what you want me to do in response. Then I can let you know specifically if it is something I can do or want to do."

Don't get stuck in the past. Arguing about who did what when is almost never constructive. Even if you do establish who did what, that still does not resolve the present problem. Refocus the discussion on the present.

"Arguing about the past isn't moving us any closer to a resolution. It just makes us both more defensive. Let's look at what we need to do to resolve the present problem."

If you are dealing with a relationship conflict, it is important to remember that you do not have to get the other party to admit they were wrong in order to have the problem resolved. If you hold on to the position that they have to eat dirt before you can let go of the grievance, you are giving them power over your life. You are saying in effect that it is up to them whether you can ever get the issue resolved. Whether you get it resolved is up to you, not them. It is your choice whether you are willing to accept the reality of what has happened and let go of it. Their admission is icing on the cake. It is not necessary.

Another response for handling Blamers is to decline their "helpful" feedback.

> "I'm not interested in what others are saying. If they have something to tell me, they can tell me directly. What I'm hearing is that you want to use hearsay to blame me. I'd like you to take responsibility for what you want to say to me."

A final response to Blamers is to confront them with your specific evidence and let them know that excuses are cheap.

> "The facts are that the machines are not working and that the job wasn't done when you promised. I want results, not excuses."

13. **Seducers**. Seducers package themselves in many interesting ways. They can be cute, helpless, nice, sexual, or complimentary. Whatever the variation, their purpose is the same. They want to trick you into giving them what they want and they do so by making you believe you're going to get something. Seductions, of course, are usually tempting. Be aware of the hidden costs before you respond. You may be paying more than it is worth to you.

a. Cute Seduction— "Wouldn't you like to help me. . . ?"
In Response: "I think I'd like to let you have the experience of doing it yourself."

b. Helpless Seduction—"I can't figure out how to make this work. Can you figure it out for me (do it for me)?"
In Response: "I'll tell you how to do it and then you can do it for yourself."

c. Sexual Seduction—"Looking for a good time?"
In Response: "I'm having a good time!"

d. Flattering Seduction—"You always do such a good job at getting things organized. No one else can do it like you do."

In Response: "Thank you, but I really don't want to take on that task again. I am willing to write out the procedure for how to do it and help brainstorm some other names."

14. **Ambiguous Abes**. Ambiguous Abes are slippery. They avoid taking responsibility or making commitments by being ambiguous, qualifying their statements, or playing the observer role.

"I might be able to."

"I'll have to think about it."

"Maybe."

"We'll see."

"I don't know for sure."

"If everything falls into place, I'll consider doing it."

"I can't say right now. Let's wait and see."

"I'll try."

In Response:

Pin them down. Point out their qualifying statements and insist on a specific response.

"I hear you being ambiguous. I want to know whether you are going to do it or not."

"When will I get a specific answer?"

"Specifically, what are you willing to commit to now?"

"I don't know what 'I'll try' means."

15. **50/50 Compromisers**. If they can't have it all, Scorekeepers resort to bargaining and 50/50 compromising. They want to ensure that they don't end up with less than 50 percent—that they get their fair share.

They will scratch your back if you'll scratch theirs. They will do you a favor and then feel you owe them one—and you can be sure they'll remind you. They'll give you this, if you'll agree to that. They'll concede on this point, if you'll concede on that one.

"It's your turn, I did it the last time."

"If they get three, we get three."

"I'll work this weekend, if you'll work next weekend."

"We'll pay for the expenses, if you'll agree to do the workshop for a reduced fee."

In Response:

Sometimes you cannot avoid getting locked into a bargaining situation. If you must bargain, be sure to do so from a Generator stance (See Chapter 11). When bargaining from a Scorekeeper stance, you are limited in your ability to accurately weigh the relative importance of issues.

Bargaining from a Generator stance, you will more accurately weigh the relative importance of issues, see the relationships between them, and assess the long-term implications of the proposed agreement.

You may be blocked on ten issues in a negotiation. As you analyze all the issues together, you may determine that only one of them is really important so you may decide to give the other party what they want on nine issues in trade for what you want on the tenth, which is the only issue that will make a difference over the long haul.

"I am willing to give you everything you want... provided I maintain exclusive rights to the contract."

16. **Complainers**. Ah! Complainers. They are a pain. They get what they want by wearing you down. The temptation is to give them what they want just so they will shut up. For Complainers, life is never fair. You never do enough for them. They always have to do more than their share, things never work out the way they expected, and they are the only ones to whom all this ever happens.

"It's not fair that they get to go first."

"How come Jan got a raise and I didn't?"

"You never buy me anything."

"I shouldn't have to do this all myself."

"How come I'm the only one who...?"

In Response:

Once again, name the game. Let them know how distasteful whining and complaining are to you. Suggest they try other options if they want a positive response.

> "I find whining and complaining annoying. It makes me want to ignore you rather than give you my attention. If you want my attention, I need you to change your behavior."

> "Your complaining feels punitive. I feel like I'm being blamed. If you're angry about something, then express it directly and tell me what you want in response."

Another response to Complainers is to refuse to take them seriously.

> "I guess you're the only one because God doesn't like you."

SUMMARY

Scorekeepers are resentful little kids in adult bodies who feel cheated or who are afraid they are not going to get enough. As a result, they have a strong sense of injustice. They are resentful and distrustful. They like to use dirty tricks and to change the rules in the middle of the game.

The primary rule for negotiating with them is to negotiate the *process* and *criteria* for settlement before talking about the specific content. The objective is to lock them into fair processes and standards before you begin.

A second response is to name their game—describe their behavior so it is public and not hidden. Strategies have power primarily because they are secret. When the strategy is exposed, it loses most of its power.

CHAPTER 7

PEACEMAKER PROFILE

Style of thinking:	Non-Critical. Idealistic. Abstract. Logical. Third-person perspective.
Way of Relating:	Interpersonal dependency. Self-conscious.
Core Needs:	Approval. Belonging. Status. To meet expectations.
Key emotions:	To be in love. Hurt. Embarrassed. Betrayed. Disappointed. Guilty.
Sense of Power:	The ability to obligate others. Officially recognized authority.
Behavior:	Avoiding anger. Keeping the peace. Taking care of everyone. Being a nice guy. Good girl. Cordial. Following the rules. Being dutiful.
Beliefs:	Anger is bad. Talking about it only makes it worse. I must have everyone's approval. Time will heal it. My worth and value depends upon what others think. There's one right answer. I can't question authority. I should...

Style of Negotiating: Deny it. Play ostrich. Accommodate. Placate. Apologize. Bring gifts. 20/80 compromise.

CHAPTER 7

PEACEMAKERS: GETTING WHAT YOU WANT THROUGH GUILT AND OBLIGATION

HOW DO YOU KNOW A PEACEMAKER?

How do you know when you or others are thinking as a Peacemaker? Well, do you ever...

- Worry about what others think of you?
- Dress so others will think well of you?
- Try to make conflicts go away?
- Say "Yes" when you want to say "No"?
- Feel like you have to take care of everyone else and no one takes care of you?
- Give advice or little speeches?
- Feel upset because no one appreciates how much you have done?
- Want a position or title because it would raise your esteem in the eyes of others?
- Give in to keep the peace?
- Try to live up to others' standards?
- Feel you don't have a right to challenge an authority figure?
- Look for the one right answer?

- Change your behavior in different situations because you think it is expected?
- Feel obligated and guilty?
- Believe someone is being nice to you even though he or she doesn't like you?
- Try to make someone else responsible for you?
- Apologize so others won't be angry with you?
- Get one negative criticism out of twenty—and feel only the negative one counts?

PEACEMAKER SCENARIOS

Here are a few examples of Peacemaker situations:

• Imagine confronting an employee about her performance. She keeps smiling and agreeing, and you know that nothing you are saying is sinking in.

• Imagine walking into your office and finding a bouquet of flowers from your boss on your desk. He hopes these will buy you off and you won't confront him for a raise.

• Imagine confronting a client who has not paid his bill because his father, the president of his company, disagrees with the charges. Your client is afraid to stand up to his father and confront him.

• Imagine settling for a 20/80 compromise just to end the conflict.

• Imagine agreeing to do something that you really don't want to do because you are afraid of displeasing someone.

• Imagine not confronting someone because you don't want to hurt their feelings.

• Imagine not taking a stand for which you might get criticized.

• Imagine liking a client from a particular ethnic group because of your personal relationship with that person. But you still feel prejudiced toward her ethnic group as a whole because you assume she's an exception.

A Peacemaker By Any Other Name

I use multiple titles to describe persons in this stage of thinking development. All are variations on the same theme. The variations include: Peacemakers, Caretakers, Earth-mothers, Godfathers, Benevolent Dictators, Perfect Pleasers, Gladhanders, Nice guys, Good Girls, Servants, Helpmates, Doormats, Ostriches, and Apologetic Accommodators.

Any of these sound vaguely familiar? What they all have in common is that they try to control others to get what they need from them by being nice and helpful and avoiding any conflict or anger. Peacemakers believe they have to earn what they want from others by taking care of others or by meeting the expectations of others. They hope that nice guys/good girls finish first.

Thinking With Your Third Eye

Sometime around junior high age, we develop the ability for third-person perspective in our thinking. This means we can step back from ourselves and consciously look at ourselves. We can think about our own thinking.

Peacemakers' thinking is not critical. They do not critically evaluate the social systems (society, family, religious tradition) in which they find themselves. They can step outside themselves but they cannot step outside their systems. They merely become conscious of themselves within their systems. They consciously adopt the beliefs and values of their systems (social authorities, parents, religious figures) and use these values to create ideal images of how the world "should" be or how people "ought" to behave.

For example:

Allen is a very pleasant purchasing agent for a sporting goods manufacturer. He is well-liked by the people within his organization, as well as by his suppliers. He is almost always friendly and listens well to others.

Raised in a lower-middle-class, white, Protestant, Republican, midwestern family, Allen lives in a ranch-style, three-bedroom home, has two children, still attends the Methodist Church, and still votes Republican. He relates to his wife and children in much the same way that his father related to his family. If you were to ask Allen who he is, he would tell you that he is a father, husband, a purchasing agent, a Republican, and a Methodist.

In short, Allen behaves and thinks much like his parents. He is living out of the values and standards he learned as a child. He believes it is important to provide his children with a stable two-parent family life and a traditional religious background. He believes it is important to be respectable, to get a good education, to work hard, and to do what's right. It matters to Allen what his parents and minister and fellow workers think of him. He does not approve of the fact that his sister decided to give her ex-husband custody of their son. It has never occurred to Allen to question or challenge any of his values.

Peacemakers are engaged in the task of developing a conscious identity. The identity they form is based on what other people, particularly authority figures, say it should be. Peacemakers consciously evaluate themselves as being good or bad, right or wrong, depending upon whether they measure up to prescribed standards.

Their identity is not the consequence of critically examined, self-appropriated values. Rather, their identity is a function of their roles (mother, husband, accountant, lawyer), their titles or status (vice-president, general manager), and what they believe significant other people expect of them. Three key characteristics of their thinking:

1. They can think from a third-person perspective. They can step back and be conscious of themselves in the world.
2. Their thinking is non-critical. They accept as truth the values given to them by authority.
3. They believe that there is an "ideal" or "right" way to be, and everyone should try to live up to these expectations.

These characteristics have several consequences when Peacemakers attempt to solve problems and resolve conflicts.

1. Because of their ability to adopt a third-person perspective, *Peacemakers are capable of abstract, rational thinking*. They can step back and consciously think about what is going on. They can follow a logical sequence of thought. They are able to stay focused and are not as easily sidetracked by diffuse factors as are Scorekeepers or Enforcers. They can recognize and disregard irrelevant issues when they are brought into a discussion. Peacemakers can think from a third-person perspective, but their third eye is a noncritical eye.
2. Because of their formulation of a conscious system of beliefs, Peacemakers are able to evaluate and judge issues and behaviors in light of their given values. Therefore, Allen is able to evaluate his sister's decisions to get a divorce and give up custody of her son in accordance with his religious and social values.

But, Peacemakers have a limitation. Since they are not able to step outside their belief system and critically evaluate it, they tend to feel that what they believe is right. If another person has a different perspective—one which doesn't fit into the Peacemaker's system of values—the other person will be judged as wrong. *Peacemakers tend to put differences into a right/wrong context.* They assume they have the truth. They become self-righteous and moralistic in a negotiation.

3. Peacemakers tend to look for the one right answer to a problem. They assume that a right answer exists and their task is to locate it. While looking for the one right answer, Peacemakers blind themselves to all the other options that may be available. In a negotiation, they will lock on to defending their "right" answer and fail to look behind their answer and objectively consider underlying needs.

For example:

Marcia and Harry run a consulting business. In an effort to reduce their printing costs, they researched various copiers.

For a long time, Harry procrastinated in making a decision because he was afraid he would make the "wrong" decision.

At home, Harry's nineteen-year-old son, Dan, decided to not go to college for a year. Dan had worked very hard in high school and had been active in sports and maintained an outside job. Now he felt burned out and wanted a year to travel, work, and save some money.

Harry wanted Dan in college and argued frequently with him. Harry couldn't really hear or accept Dan's need to kick back for a year. In Harry's mind, normal people went straight to college from high school. After all, he had.

In his arguments with Dan, Harry would fall back on his unquestioned clichés. "You're not going to make anything of yourself without a college education. If you don't go now, you'll never go. Go to school first, then take some time to play."

4. Peacemakers' ability to interpret behavior will be limited by their uncritical adherence to their personal values. They will interpret behavior in terms of their own ideal values and fail to recognize the social or environmental context out of which other behaviors derive. Peacemakers will be limited in their ability to contextually understand the behavior of others.

For example:

If I am an American, and you are a Mexican businessman, I may be unable to understand and accept your 'Mexican Standoff' pattern of negotiating. I may fail to appreciate that out of your need to not be embarrassed or wrong, you may gather all your data and then walk away from the deal without ever making an offer. If I want to make a deal with you, I am probably going to have to make the first offer.

TRYING TO KEEP EVERYONE HAPPY

Given how they think, characteristic Peacemaker behavior includes:

Anticipating expectations *Gladhanding*

Pleasing
Placating
Accommodating
Denying negative feelings
Being a benevolent dictator
Peacemaking
Entertaining
Cheerleading
Not taking a stand
Being a "Yes" person
Using clichés
Jumping in to save others
Being perfectionistic
Being a Nice Guy/Good Girl
Being a chameleon
Giving advice
Being reliable
Denying conflict
Following the rules
Denying problems
Being agreeable
Apologizing
Rationalizing
Giving in/Conceding
Asking for permission
Being helpful
Being proper
Being responsible for others

What is common among these behaviors is the Peacemaker's need to create an ideal world, to please everyone, and to avoid conflict.

What Nice Guys Are Saying To Themselves

Behind these behaviors are similar Peacemaker beliefs. Typical beliefs for Peacemakers are:

- My needs are not as important as other people's.
- I have to please everyone.
- I can't say "No."
- I have to meet expectations.
- It's important to look good.
- I do not have a right to challenge authority figures.
- I have to give them what they want so they don't get angry.
- I should...
- There's one right answer.
- If I take care of others, they'll take care of me.
- It's selfish to think of myself first.
- My role is to make everyone happy.
- It's important to act and dress appropriately.

- My worth and value depend upon what others think.
- Addressing a conflict will only make it worse.

PEACEMAKER RELATIONSHIPS: "I'LL DO ANYTHING FOR YOUR APPROVAL"

Peacemaker relationships are characterized by empathy, self-consciousness, and the need for approval. Since they are capable of stepping out of themselves with their third-person perspective, they can step into others. They are capable of knowing what others are thinking and feeling and needing. They have some capacity for empathy and therefore intimacy. They value close personal relationships.

But their relationships tend to be mutually dependent, self-conscious, caretaker relationships. The reason is simple. If they know what it is like inside others, they believe that others know what it is like inside them and they feel vulnerable and exposed. They become self-conscious. This has several consequences.

1. The opinion of other people becomes very important.
2. Peacemakers take responsibility *for* others. They may do this by taking care of others or by adopting a parental role and giving advice.
3. They value perfection. It is more important to look good than to be good. When caught in the dilemma between what needs to be done versus what will keep us in the good graces of others, the Peacemaker will be tempted to do what will make him look good. In business, Peacemakers will tend to do what will cover their fannies rather than taking a risk to do what really needs to be done.

How you dress, what you drive, who you know, where you live, what clubs you belong to, how you act—all of these are high priorities for Peacemakers. Where would big-name designers be if it weren't for Peacemakers? Somebody has to wear designer labels.

4. The behavior pattern which characterizes relationships in this level of thinking is the "Love Test Syndrome." It goes like this. We move into a new job or relationship and we immediately start anticipating what the boss or other persons expect of us. Then we do everything we can to meet those expectations.

We please them, appease them, accommodate them, apologize even if they're wrong, work overtime, do more than our share, offer to help and never express anger, no matter what. However, we all know there is no free lunch (spoken as a true Scorekeeper).

There are a few strings attached. What the Peacemaker is really doing is making payments on an insurance policy. The unconscious thinking is that, if we do all this for others now and take care of them, they will ultimately be obligated to take care of us and give us what we want.

And so the plot thickens. At some unknown point in time, we decide to set up a love test. "If they really appreciate me (love me), they'll read my mind and guess that I want... a back rub, to be taken out to dinner, a break from the kids, a raise, a new title, a promotion, a private office, a new assignment, a thank you letter, additional vacation time, or a public banquet recognizing all the contributions I have made to this organization."

Poor dumb slobs that they are, the other person always fails to read our minds accurately. They let us down, which entitles us to feel hurt, used, taken advantage of, and betrayed. "After all we did for them, those ungrateful...!" We then become martyred, complain to others, or slink back into our Scorekeeper stance and find some sneaky way to punish them. The common needs underlying these relational patterns are:

To be appreciated
To be approved of
To be recognized
To be loved
To be taken care of
To belong
To do the right thing
To be included
To look good

Given these needs, Peacemakers' favorite emotions include:

Embarrassment
Self-consciousness
Guilt
Insecurity
Frustration
Dependence
Jealousy

Feeling irritated
Feeling neglected
Feeling obligated
Feeling unappreciated
Feeling unrecognized
Feeling left out
Feeling hurt

Peacemaker Power: Obligation and Socially Sanctioned Authority

In this style of thinking, power or security comes from two sources. The first is our ability to obligate others to be or do what we want. The second resides in socially approved authority figures.

Caretaking and pleasing others, variations of the Peacemaker theme, are subtle ways to control and manipulate them. As Caretakers, power stems from how effective we are at making others feel obligated and guilty. We've been so good to them and we are such nice guys (good girls), how could they not give us what we want? People who fail to be sufficiently obligated and guilty are judged to be either selfish or lazy.

The second source of power for Peacemakers is official authority. Peacemakers assume that, if the other person has the proper credentials, titles, degrees, or position, he must know more. Peacemakers assume that their parents, religious leaders, physicians, therapists, political leaders, insurance agent, and hairdresser all know more about what is good for them than they know themselves.

It is as if Peacemakers assume that a preordained, defined body of truth exists "out there" somewhere and that authority figures are the only ones who have access to it. Therefore, even though they may resent what authority figures say or do, Peacemakers do not believe they have a right to question or challenge those authorities.

For example:

A few years ago, I was serving as a consultant for a community action agency. The county commissioners had cut the agency's budget and it was unlikely that the agency would be able to survive. I lobbied with the director of the agency to challenge the commissioners' decision. Her response: "We can't do that. They're the county commissioners. They obviously have a broader picture of the needs of the county than I do."

Peacemaker thinking is a source of security and consolation. Assuming that someone out there has the truth means there are a lot of things we don't have to worry about. We don't have to worry about social or political or economic issues because people in official positions who know more than we do are taking care of those problems. Even if we don't understand something, someone out there does. We don't have to worry.

At the same time, when we want to do something, we can go to a person in authority and ask his or her permission. If they are "into" their roles, they can take care of us by giving us permission and telling us how to do whatever it is we want to do. Then, if we screw up, it's not our fault: they told us to do it.

It's a nice system, as long as it works. The only problem is that we are not free to think for ourselves, to question or challenge, or to do what may feel right to us. Our obligation as Peacemakers is to keep the status quo going and to fit into the program.

Implications for Negotiating from a Peacemaker Stance

When it comes to negotiating, Peacemakers do a better job of solving problems than Enforcers or Scorekeepers, but they are not significantly better at resolving conflicts. Their capacity for abstract rational thinking enables them to analyze problems, to plan for a negotiation, and to participate in long-range planning—without having concrete data immediately before them.

However, when a conflict arises, Peacemakers play ostrich. Because of their need to have everyone like them, Peacemakers do anything they can to make the conflict go away rather than resolve it. They are afraid that if they attempt to address the negative issues in the relationship, someone might get angry with them and disapprove.

While this style of thinking begins in early adolescence, many adults have never developed beyond this stage of functioning. Being a Peacemaker has been the norm for what it means to be an adult. Our models for negotiating, especially in our personal lives, have been Peacemaker models. We see Peacemaker negotiators in:

The staff person who denies (with locked jaw) he or she is angry.

The employee who agrees with all the negative feedback you are giving her. (Your assumption is that she just wants to make this interview go away.)

The client who keeps focusing on solving the problem and avoids talking about the conflicts in your relationship.

The employees who keep asking you to clarify your expectations of them.

The staff person who is always agreeable and never takes an unpopular stand.

Some Specific Implications

1. As a Peacemaker, you will be able to think in abstract, rational terms. You will be able to theorize about the causes of a problem and speculate (in your head) on possible solutions. However, you will have a tendency to look for the one right answer and ignore all the potential options available.

Often, you will be indecisive or procrastinate because you are afraid you will make the wrong decision. You are more concerned about what others will think than what needs to be done.

2. You will have some capacity for empathy—to understand the other person's perspective and the needs being

expressed by his behavior. This will be especially true for people who are like you.

You'll find it easier to understand others who work with you or look like you or come from the same ethnic background. If you are both in the marketing department, you will find it easy to understand each other but hard to understand the people in production.

3. You will establish more productive relationships with others than with Enforcers or Scorekeepers. You will be more trusting, less paranoid, less afraid of being cheated. People will describe you as friendly and easy-going.

4. You will be able to solve problems but not resolve conflicts. You will avoid conflicts by playing ostrich. You will attempt to calm any expression of anger. You will play the Peacemaker role—attempting to keep everyone happy. You'll deny your own anger.

5. You will concede or give in to please others and make uncomfortable feelings go away. You will settle for a 20/80 compromise, giving the other person 80 percent if he won't be angry. Later on, of course, you will resent him for having taken advantage of you.

(Many divorces get settled this way. "I was tired of fighting. I just wanted to get it over with.")

6. You will apologize even when you're right. You hope that if you apologize, they'll drop the matter and you won't have to deal with it.

7. When you do not agree with authority figures, you'll be accommodating to their face but you'll go off feeling resentful and complaining to others. We see examples of this with employees who don't raise objections with their boss in a meeting,but then they go back to their department and complain to fellow employees.

8. You will be able to step back from your experience and reflect upon it. As a result, you will be more accurate than Scorekeepers in your perceptions and you will be

more aware of the process going on in addition to the content of the discussion.

9. You will tend to judge others as being wrong or selfish if they do not fit into your value system.

10. Your future solutions will tend to be idealizations of your values rather than innovative and different. Your solutions will also tend to be the kind which will enable you to go back home to your constituency and look good in their eyes.

If Peacemakers are this "helpful," how do you negotiate with them? Options for negotiating with Peacemakers are outlined in the next chapter.

CHAPTER 8

PACIFYING THE PEACEMAKER

Recall that Peacemakers are concerned about what other people think of them. They need to look good and meet everyone's expectations. They are uncomfortable if anyone gets angry with them or disapproves. They work hard to keep the peace, to calm the waters, to make everyone happy.

When it comes to conflict, Peacemakers play ostrich. They do everything they can to make a conflict go away rather than face it. When it comes to problem-solving, they will avoid anything that might make them look bad.

The basic philosophy of the Peacemaker is that nice guys finish first. They believe that if they can keep everyone happy and avoid any real confrontation, others will feel obligated to give them what they want. After all, why wouldn't you? They're so nice.

When responding to Peacemakers, the objective is to not let them slip out and disappear or buy you off with their niceness. You need to gently and firmly pull the ostrich's head out of the ground and get him to look at you, eyeball to eyeball.

Or, as a client once described the process, it is like being skillful with a caulking gun. You have to keep plugging up the holes through which Peacemakers try to sneak.

Peacemakers are tough to confront. They shift the responsibility onto you. They make you feel guilty for confronting them. They are masters at making others feel afraid of hurting their feelings.

In the following examples, you'll recognize some commonalities and overlapping. This is due to an overall behavior sequence which is described in Chapter 7 as the Love Test Syndrome. The different Peacemaker examples represent the various roles people adopt as they carry out the steps in the Love Test Syndrome sequence.

1. **Deniers.** Deniers try to make you go away by denying they have a problem or conflict. Or they deny that they just stuck a knife in your back. Peacemakers, like everyone else, get angry, but they are afraid to show their anger directly. They will "get" you nicely and then, when they are confronted, deny that they meant anything by their behavior.

You can usually tell when someone is denying by the incongruity between their words and their behavior or by the tone of their voice.

"I don't know what you're talking about."
"What do you mean? I wouldn't do that!"
"I'm not angry!" (In an irritated tone of voice)
"It's no big deal. No problem."
"I can handle it."
"I never intended to hurt you."

In Response:

Don't let them buy you off with their denials. If they deny they have a problem, tell them you have one and you need their help to resolve it. Consider what conditions they might need to feel safe enough to negotiate openly and directly with you.

If the Denier is persistent in his or her denial, be equally persistent in your response. Point out the behavioral data from which you are responding. Especially point out the incongruities you perceive in his behavior.

"I believe you when you say that you don't have a problem. Unfortunately, I do, and it involves you. I need your cooperation to get it resolved."

"If you don't know what I am talking about, let me explain. When I came to work, the lights were on, the typewriter was running, and the door was unlocked.

Unless I'm mistaken, you were the last one to leave here yesterday. That makes me assume you're responsible."

"I hear you say you're not angry, but your voice sounds angry. I'm getting a double message."

2. **The Guilty Ones/Apologizers.** Guilty Ones take the blame upon themselves for whatever has happened in order to make it go away. They are quick to apologize, hoping that their apology will buy you off and you will drop the issue. Be aware that the flip side of guilt is resentment. Apologetic people are resentful people who are afraid of their own anger and yours. They do whatever they can to avoid angry confrontations.

"I was probably the last one to use it."

"I'm sorry I'm late."

"No, no. That was my fault. I shouldn't have said the things I said."

In Response:

Do not allow them to take all the blame. They may apologize now, but that resolves nothing. It is helpful to distinguish between healing apologies and avoiding apologies. In a healing apology, you will experience direct contact and congruence with the other person. You will feel resolved.

With an avoiding apology, something will be missing. You will feel as if you are being bought off. You will not feel resolved, and you will probably not be clear as to what it is they intend to do differently. You'll have the sense that you're going to repeat the cycle again.

"I appreciate your apology, but making you feel guilty is not why I raised the issue. I don't want to blame anyone. I want to solve the problem so it doesn't happen again."

"Yes, you are late again and I need to talk about that. That happens often when we have appointments with each other. It makes me feel I'm not very important or my time isn't valued. I'd like a commitment from you that you'll be on time in the future."

"I don't want you to take all the blame. We have both

contributed to the conflict. I want us to step back and look at what we each have done and own responsibility for our part of it—and I want to resolve the underlying issues. I don't want to go through this again. And I don't want you to go away feeling resentful so that I have to pay a price later."

3. **Accommodators.** Accommodators adapt to satisfy others. They will agree to anything just to keep the peace—and to obligate others. They hope that if they are self-effacing now, you'll feel responsible for them later. They give you what you want now. Later, you will be expected to read their minds and guess what they want.

"I don't mind."
"No, go ahead. I'll wait."
"Do what you want."
"My plans aren't important."
"That's OK. We'll do it your way."

In Response:

Be aware of the price you may have to pay later. Don't let them do more than they really want to do unless you enjoy being obligated.

"I appreciate your generosity. However, I want to insure that you are not doing more than you really want to do. I don't want to feel obligated."

"When you are self-effacing, I get worried about paying a price for your resentment later on."

4. **Placaters, Appeasers, and Conceders.** These people try to calm the waters by appeasing and pacifying. They will soothe or mollify by making concessions and often will sacrifice principles. They will be 20/80 compromisers. They'll take 20 percent and give you 80 percent, if that will pacify you and get rid of the immediate discomfort. Then they go away and resent you for having taken advantage of them.

"Tell me what you want and I'll give it to you. Just don't stay angry with me."

"It doesn't do any good to argue. Let's not raise our voices. Anger never solved anything. It only makes matters worse."

"You can have everything else. Just give me the old pick-up."

"If you will just handle the arrangements, I'll do all the rest."

In Response:

Don't let them give in or pour oil on the water. Insist on equal distribution of goods and tasks. Ensure that it is a fair settlement or division, otherwise you will be making long-term payments. Make sure you are emotionally committed to the underlying standards and desired results. Refuse to be mollified. Anger doesn't kill relationships—it is what you do not talk about and resolve that destroys relationships.

"I don't want you to just give in to me."

"I think it is important that we establish fair criteria so neither of us feels resentful later."

"I don't want you to have to do it all. I want to do my fair share so we can both feel good about it."

"I'm not willing to stuff my anger and pretend everything is OK when it isn't. We need to talk about what's going on between us and try to understand it so we can get some resolution."

5. **Pleasers.** Pleasers hope that if they are nice enough, you will feel too guilty to confront them. They will be pleasant, never show their anger directly, smile a lot, and stay superficial. They are often complimentary and charming. They are great "Gladhandlers"—one of the "good ole boys" who'll slap you on the back. It is important to them to look good and to please everyone by meeting their expectations. At their sweetest, you can pour them on pancakes.

"Well, it's great to see you again. It's been a long time. How is Molly? How's the family?"

"You do such a wonderful job at that. Everyone says so."

In Response:

Point out the double binds, help them look good, and be persistent.

> "It's great to see you too, because I have some things I need to talk about with you. It's difficult for me to confront you because you are always so nice. I'm afraid of hurting your feelings but I don't want my fear to prevent me from addressing the conflict I have with you."

> "I appreciate your compliments, but your compliments make it harder for me to do what I need to do right now. I feel caught in a double bind. If I confront you, I must be an insensitive, ungrateful person, but I do need to confront you. We need to talk."

6. **Helpful Harriets (Earthmothers, Godfathers, Caretakers)**
These people love to take care of you. They will do favors for you, run errands for you, offer to help, work overtime, take on more than their share—anticipate your every need.

However, this helpful caretaking is not free. They have a hidden agenda. They're taking care of you now, but ultimately you're supposed to take care of them.

They are building an insurance policy to be cashed in at some later date. AND, after all they've done for you, you certainly would not be so ungrateful as to confront them or hold them accountable.

> "I'll work on the weekend so the others can take off."

> "I think I deserve a raise after all I've done."

In Response:

Don't be bought off. Make it clear that you do not want them to do more than they really want to do. You do not owe anyone anything. This does not mean you are a crass Scorekeeper getting whatever you can out of everyone. It means that no one has the right to secretly obligate you into owing them something or into being responsible for them.

To freely want to be generous to others because they have freely been generous with you is different than being obligated and responding out of a sense of duty. Dutiful obligation breeds resentment and is not constructive for either party.

> "I appreciate all you've done for me personally and for the company. You've done a fine job and I want to keep you. However, there simply is not money in the budget right now for additional raises. I am willing to review this with you again in three months when we may be in a stronger financial position."

> "I'm concerned that you are doing more than you really want to do. I want you to respect your own boundaries so you don't feel taken advantage of later."

> "While I'm grateful for all you've done, we still have a problem to resolve."

7. **Wounded Animals.** Wounded Animals get hurt. This is the posture Caretakers frequently take when they decide to cash in their insurance policy. They become martyrs to make you feel guilty. They hope that your guilt will make you back off. They can then avoid being responsible for their actions.

> "How could you say that after all I've done for you?"

> "I did the best I could."

> "I was only trying to do what I thought was best for you."

> "Well, if that's how you feel. . ." (hurt silence)

In Response:

Point out the double bind their "hurtness" puts you in and decline to buy into it. Be specific about describing their martyred behavior. Don't blame them but insist that they own responsibility for their behavior. If you are not specific in describing their behavior, they will probably deny it or become confused.

> "When you say that and act hurt, the message I get is that I don't have a right to respond."

> "All that you have done for me does not negate what you also did *to* me. Ignoring my feelings is not going to

resolve the conflict. You feeling hurt and me feeling guilty doesn't help us move on."

"I believe you did the best you could. I also know what my experience has been. Even though you did the best you could, I also have some anger and sadness about some of what you did—and didn't do. And I need to get that resolved with you."

"That is how I feel and I want to talk about it. I'm not willing to be dismissed because you feel hurt. I want you to understand what I am feeling and needing and what I want from you in response."

8. **Naggers.** Naggers are a variation of Martyrs, Complainers, Jailers, and Blamers. Naggers do more than simply ask for what they want. They have a way of sticking a knife in you and making you cringe while they make their requests. They frequently repeat themselves, and they are fond of asking questions instead of making statements. Their questions have a hook in them—an underlying punitive message.

Nagging is a favorite behavior of Caretakers who feel resentful for all they have done in the past. They are indirectly expressing their anger and hoping to make you pay. They are big on reminding you of your obligations and past promises.

"When are you going to finish cleaning the supply closets like you *promised*?"
"*How many times* do I have to remind you?"
"The job *still* isn't finished."

In Response:

Refuse to be punished and held to past agreements that are no longer applicable. Point out the punitive knife in their message and address the underlying conflict.

"You're right. I did promise to do that. However, at the time that I agreed we had not completed the inventory. Our situation is different now."

"Your tone of voice and words this time tell me that you're feeling resentful. We obviously have a conflict we need to address. Tell me what you are feeling."

"Your use of the word 'still' makes me feel as if I'm being punished. I'm not willing to be punished. I am willing to listen to what you're feeling and needing. I'd like to resolve whatever the conflict is between us."

SIX POINTS FOR PACIFYING PEACEMAKERS

Remember:

1. If you are not their parent, and if they are not still a child, then you are not responsible for them. *No one has the right to make you feel guilty and obligated.*
2. Because they feel *'hurt'* does not mean:
   - It is your fault.
   - They are weak and helpless.
   - They will be devastated and die if you confront them.
3. Peacemakers have a lot of power in their niceness. Don't buy into it and give your power away.
4. Be aware of all the variations of hidden Peacemaker anger. It has a way of getting you before you know you've been gotten.

   Examples of hidden Peacemaker anger include:
   - Being hurt
   - Being disappointed
   - Being shy
   - Being overly nice or helpful
   - Incongruent messages
   - Denial
5. Be persistent. Tell them how difficult it is to confront them and stay with it.
6. Listen for the incongruity between what their words are saying and what their behavior or voice tone is saying. Point out the incongruity.

CHAPTER 9

REBEL PRODUCER PROFILE

Style of Thinking:	Either/Or. Focus on differences.
Way of Relating:	Arm's length. Independently. Avoiding commitment.
Core Needs:	To prove competence and autonomy. To be free.
Key Emotions:	Excitement and fear. Determination. Impatience.
Sense of Power:	In being competent and producing results.
Behavior:	Entrepreneurial. Challenging authority and institutions. Superior. Tough. Pragmatic. Abrupt. Task-oriented. Serious and down to business. Refusing to justify themselves. Shaping up or reforming.
Beliefs:	I'll show them I can take care of myself. I have to prove myself. If I don't stay tough, I'll lose my autonomy. I don't have time to deal with people.

Style of Negotiating: Tough. Focused on differences. Argumentative. Result-oriented with problems while avoiding conflicts. Superior. Dismissing. Arrogant. Sarcastic. Pragmatic compromises.

CHAPTER 9

REBEL PRODUCERS: GETTING WHAT YOU WANT BY DOING IT YOURSELF

We've described Enforcers, Scorekeepers, and Peacemakers–three different levels of thinking that you encounter in your negotiations. Rebel Producers are a fourth type.

How do you know when you are dealing with a Rebel Producer? Well, have you ever...

- Felt as if you were leaving home?
- Felt impatient because you wanted results, now?
- Refused to justify yourself?
- Enjoyed telling someone "No"?
- Acted tough so you could feel stronger?
- Wanted to be recognized for who you were as a person, not for your roles?
- Felt the need to prove yourself?
- Dismissed others to put them off?
- Refused to follow the program?
- Felt caught between two extreme positions?
- Wanted to shape someone up?
- Been civilly disobedient?
- Felt the need to keep others at arm's length–to not be fenced in or to give yourself away?
- Been accused of being stubborn?
- Acted superior or arrogant?

- Became anxious when you couldn't make things happen?
- Believed that your power depended on your expertise?

I WANNA BE MY OWN PERSON

As the name implies, Rebel Producers are rebellious and productive. They are former Peacemakers who have tired of trying to meet everyone else's expectations. They are tired of giving up what they want to keep everyone else happy. They resent being defined by their roles. They have decided the price for having everyone's approval is too high.

So they rebel and leave home. Their basic posture is to dismiss others and set out to prove they can do it themselves and make it on their own. Their goal is to prove they can be independent, autonomous adults. They do this by proving they can be productive and make things happen.

Rebel Producers are caught in a dilemma. On one hand, they want to be independent and autonomous; on the other hand, they would like to be liked. On one hand, they feel excited about exploring, about creating new possibilities for their lives. On the other hand, they are afraid they aren't enough to make it on their own.

Rebel Producers are experimenting with who they can be in the world. If they don't know who they can be, they do know what they don't want to be. They don't want to be dependent and accommodating. They don't want to have to please everyone else and rigidly follow the program. They don't want to be committed and tied down and trapped. They don't want to be Peacemakers.

So they begin to define themselves in negative terms—in terms of what they do not want to be. They begin to achieve definition by pushing against former authority figures and limiting structures.

Many people move into this level during their late teens or early adult years. The shift into a Rebel Producer style of thinking usually requires some distancing from former authority and the decision to become personally responsible for their own lives. Typically, this occurs during their college years.

In the past, women might move into Rebel Producer capacities during college, but frequently would then revert back to Peacemaker thinking, especially if they did not develop careers. Men, on the other hand, tended more often to move into Rebel Producer thinking in their professional lives but would operate from Peacemaker thinking in their personal lives.

All this has changed since the 1960s. We have gone through a major cultural revolution which has resulted in a shift in the social norm for adult capacities for thinking and relating.

We see this in all the 'rights' movements—civil rights, Gray Panthers, Gay Power, the women's movement. We see the shift also in the protests against armed conflict beginning with Vietnam, the increase in divorce rates, the changes that have occurred in mainstream organized religions (i.e., the Roman Catholic Church's Second Vatican Council), and so on.

The result is that more men and women in the twenty to fifty-year age group are functioning from Rebel Producer thinking. They include:

> The single parent proving she can support herself and her children.
>
> The professional man building his career.
>
> The professional woman who holds a top management position in what was previously a male-dominated business.
>
> The number of couples who choose to live together without getting married.
>
> The entrepreneur who puts himself out on a limb and then scrambles to build a platform to stay there.

You will encounter this tough and independent person more frequently in negotiations than you would have twenty years ago. The common needs of Rebel Producers are:

To be respected	To be competent
To be self-sufficient	To achieve results

To prove themselves

Given these needs, familiar emotions for Rebel Producers include:

Loneliness
Impatience
Anger
Indignation
Resistance
Tough Resignation
Determination
Excitement
Superiority
Fear
Hopefulness
Weariness
Antsy-ness
Toughness

Rebel Producer Scenarios

Imagine yourself sitting down with the company controller. She is attired in her "dress for success" blue suit with a little silk tie. She looks friendly enough, but when you ask her to explain why something happened, she refuses to justify herself.

Imagine yourself telling your partner you need a report completed; he gives you a look of dismissal and walks away without saying anything.

Imagine yourself wondering where your secretary is. She has a habit of not coming to work on time and not letting you know when she won't be there. She doesn't like being tied down to a rigid schedule.

Imagine yourself confronting an employee about his performance. He responds indignantly that he gets his work done and he doesn't need a parent telling him what to do or how to do it.

Imagine yourself trying to get a client to make a commitment while he stalls for more time because he doesn't want to be pinned down.

Imagine yourself asking your boss if you can try out a new idea, and his response is "No" because, "We've never done it that way before." You, in turn, challenge him to justify his position.

Imagine yourself trying to return a defective product you have recently purchased. Since you don't have your receipt, you are told the store cannot take it back because, "It is against store policy." You get impatient and angry and ask to see the manager. The manager appears and you challenge the store policy.

Imagine yourself calling a female client to make a lunch appointment. She is the first woman foreperson in her company. While still on the phone, she lets you know in a firm voice that she is happily married, and she will pay for her own lunch.

Rebel Producers tend to use either/or thinking. This is partly a function of their need to define themselves by pushing against others. They define themselves by taking extreme or polar positions. "Either my boss is right or I am right; we can't both be right."

In their relationships with others, Rebel Producers tend to keep others at arms' length and to avoid personal commitments. They are afraid of being sucked in and dependent again as they were when they functioned as Peacemakers.

Their source of power resides in how tough they can be and in what they can produce. They will tend to distrust traditional authority. Rather, they will respect people who can get the job done—whatever their status or title might be.

I Believe I Can

Common beliefs of Rebel Producers include:

- I can take care of myself.
- Why should I? They can't make me do it!
- Commitment equals giving myself away.
- I have to prove myself.
- I'll show them.
- I have to stay tough to keep from giving myself away.
- I don't have time to relax or play.
- I don't have time to deal with people problems.
- If I want it done right, I'll have to do it myself.
- I'm superior—I hope.
- I need to shape up and get on with it.

- I don't need anyone to tell me how to do it.

Characteristic of these beliefs is the Rebel Producers' need to prove they are tough, competent, and can make it on their own.

EITHER/OR THINKING

Rebel Producers, in their need to be productive and to prove themselves, are 'results' oriented. "I don't want excuses. I want results!" Rebel Producers are capable of analyzing a full-blown idea for its practical implications. They will define a problem logically, set goals, and develop plans to achieve practical results.

They will be impatient with others who are not producing. They are focused, directional, alert, disciplined, incisive, and energetic. They move with a purpose. They want to get the job done. "I want this wrapped up before we leave here today. If it's not done today, you'll need to come in tomorrow morning (Saturday) and finish it."

Rebel Producers will be more convinced by empirical evidence and logic than by theories or authority. While they refuse to justify themselves, they expect everyone else to justify themselves. They need to be convinced with hard facts. Their attitude is "Prove it to me!" "Show me!" "Put up or shut up!"

Because of their dichotomous thinking, Rebel Producers focus on differences between items rather than on similarities. They will tend to perceive issues as polar extremes. This is a limitation in their problem-solving capability. They will be likely to jump to solutions in their impatience to get things done, and the solutions they identify will be polar extremes—neither of which are very appealing. Rebel Producers sometimes fail to see all the gray areas between the black and white.

For example:

As a CPA, Jonathan was extremely dissatisfied with his partnership. The other partners were riding on old clients and were not motivated in making the firm grow. Jonathan raised his concerns, but no one seemed to listen, and he felt increasing internal pressure to move on.

Then a larger firm inquired whether Jonathan might be interested in joining as a partner. Jonathan was excited about the offer. It would be his way out. But his excitement quickly turned to frustration and anger during the first negotiation meeting. The new firm was not willing to take Jonathan on as a full partner until after a year's trial period, and the salary offer was too low.

Jonathan felt stuck. He believed he had only two options, and neither one felt feasible. In reality, as he learned a few weeks later, he had other options. He was able to negotiate a full partnership for a higher salary with a third firm. But, at the time of the first negotiation, Jonathan was stuck in Rebel Producer dichotomous thinking and could see only two extreme options.

Rebel Producers focus on differences. This allows them to challenge, to push against, and to be superior. But often this attitude creates unnecessary conflicts. They fail to see what they have in common with the other person. Often they focus more on what they disagree about rather than looking for overlapping areas of agreement.

On the other hand, the single-mindedness of Rebel Producers keeps them on track. Determined and persistent, they are not easily diverted from their goals.

For example:

Roger and Ann work together. Roger is trying to describe to Ann his experience in attempting to solve problems with her. He describes the fact that whenever he tells her that he needs her help, she immediately assumes he is criticizing her for not having done enough and therefore gets defensive and justifies herself. This usually results in Roger getting tired and dismissing her with "Just forget it." Roger wants them to both understand the pattern so they can work together to change it.

True to form, Ann gets defensive and starts justifying what she did in a meeting yesterday, and Roger, being focused, does not allow himself to get sidetracked and keeps bringing her back to the core issue: the typical pattern between them which they are engaged in right now.

So he says to Ann: "The meeting yesterday is just one example. What we are doing right now is another example. I don't want to get sidetracked into arguing over particular examples. I want to step back from them and try to understand the repeating pattern we are in." And then, as a true Rebel Producer, he slips in a little, superior, sarcastic gotcha: "If you can manage to stay focused!"

Rebel Producers are more capable of seeing a whole picture because they are less encumbered by their former prejudices. They are less likely to filter out what doesn't fit into their preconceived beliefs and values about how things should be. They are less judgmental. They can step outside their systems and accept things as they are. A person in this stage can still value lifelong commitments and, at the same time, understand and accept that people have valid reasons for getting divorced.

Along the same line, Rebel Producers will be creative and diffuse since they are willing to try out and experiment with innovative ideas. They will turn problems inside out and upside down to gain fresh insights. They are free to dream. Their posture will be "Why not?" As one office equipment sales manager said: "If you want to motivate me, just tell me I can't do it. I guarantee I'll find some way to get it done just to prove you're wrong."

Rebel Producers will also be more open-minded and less judgmental in their brainstorming. They will defocus and flash back, reverse their thought process to experience what happened in the past. They will also flash forward, anticipating visually what might happen and what they will feel in that future situation. This enables them to anticipate creatively the responses of others and to prepare for future negotiations.

For example:

Kay had not been separated long from her husband and still felt awkward about dating. When Morris asked her to go to San Francisco for the weekend, she said she had to think about it. She felt torn.

She liked Morris and didn't want him to go away, but she also did not feel ready to be sexually intimate with someone. She pictured the two of them in San Francisco together—walking along the wharf, having dinner—it felt like fun. Then she pictured them together in the motel, and she knew she couldn't do it.

In the past (as a Peacemaker), Kay would have made some excuse. This time she told the truth, that it scared her and she didn't want to feel used. "I wish I could have told him without my voice sounding so tough, but at least I said it. After getting a picture of us in the motel, I knew that even if I never saw him again, I had to say 'no.'"

Rebel Producers take stands and say "no." They will be less competitive than Scorekeepers, but they will probably be perceived as being more competitive than Peacemakers. They are really competitive with themselves, which stems from their need to prove to themselves what they can do. This may be reflected in the number of people jogging today as opposed to participating in competitive sports.

Relationships: "I'll Do It Myself, Thank You"

Relationships for Rebel Producers will tend to be at arm's length and above it all. This is the stage in which people decide to get divorces, to move into new careers, or to start their own businesses.

Rebel Producers do not like to be told what to do and how to do it. If you want to motivate a Rebel Producer, give her a task and set her free to do it in her own way at her own pace. "Just tell me what you want done. I can figure out how to do it for myself."

Rebel Producers tend to be independent loners. If they want something done, they are more likely to do it themselves rather than ask for help. They don't want to take a chance on being told "no," and they don't want to mess around waiting for other people to get their act together. "If you want something done, you've got to do it yourself."

Or as one vice-president said in regard to his poor relationship with his union workers: "I don't have the time or the inclination to sit around talking about our relationship. We've got quotas to meet."

If confronted, Rebel Producers will probably become indignant and refuse to justify themselves. They have difficulty distinguishing between explaining themselves as adults so others can understand them and having to justify themselves to get approval, like children. They are also likely to act superior and dismissive, as if it is beneath them to have to explain themselves. "I don't owe you any explanation. It's none of your business. Who do you think you are?"

Rebel Producers will be reformers and fixers. They believe it is their responsibility to challenge traditional authority and traditional ways of doing things. They are adamant about shaping up everyone and everything. "We don't have time to sit around feeling sorry for ourselves. Shape up and get back to work."

If you can stand all their reformer tendencies, they are useful and productive workers. They get a lot done—antagonizing people along the way. They make good project leaders, but not very good supervisors and mentors.

For example:

One corporate president wondered why his people distrusted and resented him. The first thing we noticed was that he addressed them by their childhood nicknames: Tommy, Jimmy, Bobby—a subtle way to be superior. The second thing we noticed was that when the foreman asked him what he wanted from the foreman's crew (they had been arguing over the time-line for a project), the president's immediate response was: "I don't want anything from you. This company will be here long after you're gone, Jimmy." After he had succeeded in antagonizing his foreman, the president went on to list the six things he needed from the foreman's crew. He didn't understand why the foreman was so hostile and non-cooperative.

Typical behavior for Rebel Producers includes:

Being belligerent
Acting tough
Dismissing
Refusing to justify
Civilly disobeying
Gathering data
Exploring and Experimenting
Challenging
Erupting in anger
Solving problems
Being efficient
Being determined
Being negative
Using sarcasm
Being independent
Avoiding commitment

Refusing to explain actions
Requiring proof
Being pragmatic
Taking either/or positions
Rejecting traditional authority
Debating
Being understanding
Being self-sufficient
Being above it all
Thinking in binary terms (either/or)
Proving myself
Leaving home
Being superior
Working ceaselessly
Being goal-oriented
Requiring proof
Staying distant
Compartmentalizing
Being stubborn

REBEL PRODUCER POWER: "I'LL SHOW YOU"

The power of Rebel Producers resides first in their ability to be tough and independent and productive. As former Peacemakers, they have learned that when they get angry they feel stronger. Their anger allows them to objectify others and to put a protective boundary around themselves. As long as they are angry, they can stay tough and push away more vulnerable feelings. They don't have to feel others' pain as much.

So Rebel Producers put a premium on staying tough and superior. They are often afraid to be gentle or to let down their guard for fear others will see them as being weak. In their polarized, either/or thinking, they are also afraid that if they aren't tough all the time, they will become helpless and dependent.

For example:

Hilda ran her own employment agency. She was determined to show her former husband that she could be more successful than he at his own business. She had a reputation for being demanding. During a six-month period, she hired and fired twenty-two employees. When her business went bankrupt during the recession, a newspaper columnist included a sarcastic paragraph in his weekly "news items" that there was going to be a party of all her former employees in the local sports stadium. Hilda had been a tough employer. Her employees either produced immediate results or they went looking for another job.

The other source of power for Rebel Producers is charismatic leaders. While they dismiss traditional authority figures, Rebel Producers are not always sure they know enough to trust their own truth. Therefore, they go looking for some new charismatic leader who might possess the truth.

Implications For Negotiating From A Rebel Producer Stance

When it comes to negotiating, Rebel Producers have more advantages and fewer liabilities. On the positive side, their ability to step outside themselves and their traditional systems empowers them to see a more complex, complete picture.

The questioning and challenging done by Rebel Producers not only helps them to see more of what exists and to see through more, but also helps them generate more innovative solutions. Their reduced prejudice and subsequently enhanced insight into others enables them to be more objective. Their pragmatic single-mindedness helps them to avoid getting caught in lower-level game-playing.

On the negative side, Rebel Producers' dichotomous thinking causes them to limit their options unnecessarily. Their need to act tough and to stay angry in order to feel strong creates unnecessary conflicts with others and often prevents them from resolving conflicts. The same is true of their need to prove themselves and their subsequent impatience and superior attitude.

We see Rebel Producers in:

- The partner who refuses to give you the satisfaction of letting you know what he intends to do and when. The silent message: "I'll do it, but it will be on my terms."
- The woman executive who has to act tough to compete in a male-dominated environment.
- The male executive who sits across the table from you with his arms folded across his chest and a superior, distant look on his face that says "Show me."

- The rising young employee who pushes against his superiors by challenging the ways things have been done in the past. When you confront him, he is likely to become argumentative and insistent, expecting you to justify yourself.
- The client who when confronted dismisses you and states that, "I don't need you and don't have to put up with this!"
- The staff member who always disagrees with you, before making a statement which actually builds upon what you just said.

As a Rebel Producer, you will have certain key abilities and disabilities:

1. You will be able to use your abstract, rational, analytical capacities to pragmatically solve problems and plan for negotiations. For example, you will be able to think critically and to look objectively at data instead of simply hoping everything will work out.
2. You will have enhanced empathy for others who are different from you. You may begin to accept the fact that people live different life-styles.
3. At the same time, your superior, arrogant, dismissing, and impatient behavior will antagonize others and create unnecessary conflicts. Your need to be tough all the time will prevent you from taking others in so conflicts can be resolved. You will unnecessarily pit yourself against others.
4. Similarly, your tendency to push against others will antagonize and overwhelm them. You will sometimes use a two-by-four when a gentle confrontation would be more effective.
5. Your tendency to focus on the differences and what is wrong rather than the similarities will keep others separate from you and the problem or conflict unresolved.
6. Your dichotomous, either/or thinking will limit your ability to see all the possible solutions. In the face of a conflict, you will tend to collapse in extreme posi-

tions—either holding tough and stubborn or caving in and conceding.

7. You will confuse the difference between explaining yourself and justifying yourself. As a result, others will sometimes make false assumptions about your intentions.
8. You will be more convinced by empirical evidence than emotional persuasion.
9. Your determination and persistence will keep you on track until you get satisfactory results. Your single-mindedness will help you to attend to what is immediately, obviously going on.
10. Less limited by previous prejudices, you will see more interrelated factors in a whole situation.
11. You will be more willing to try out innovative solutions.
12. Your need to prove yourself will sometimes set you up to beat other people rather than understand them—and if you don't beat them, you'll likely try to shape them up.
13. You will be able to maintain more of an objective distance. By stepping back and observing what is going on, you will be more able to separate the problem being discussed from relationship issues.

Rebel Producers make tough negotiators. That's good for solving problems, but not so good for solving conflicts. As we have seen in each of the lower levels—Enforcers, Scorekeepers, Peacemakers, and Rebel Producers—problems can be negotiated more or less effectively, but relationship conflicts cannot be resolved. Only on the next level, Generators, (described in Chapter 11) can we successfully negotiate problems and conflicts.

How do you negotiate with a Rebel Producer? That question is answered in the next chapter.

CHAPTER 10

TAKING ON THE TOUGH GUYS

Rebel Producers work hard to be independent and to prove they can take care of themselves. They want to do things their own way. They don't want to have to answer to anyone. Their tendency is to overstate their toughness and competence in order to protect themselves.

Rebel Producers use tactics that allow them to keep at a distance and to put the opposition off and down. They love to throw others off balance by acting tough. They will act superior and above it all and dismissive. They'll keep busy to keep others away. And, while they will refuse to justify themselves, they will challenge others to justify and prove their positions.

The external behavior of Rebel Producers is sometimes difficult to distinguish from Enforcer behavior. The difference is that Rebel Producers are not primarily trying to punish or beat others. They are simply trying to maintain their own ground and accomplishments. The behavioral clues are that Rebel Producers tend to be calmer, analytical, cool, and superior. They sound like defensive and rebellious teenagers rather than bullies.

In general, the best response for dealing with Rebel Producers is to try to melt them. Instead of pushing back, invite them to work with you. Instead of dismissing their behavior, use their forceful energy to generate better and more creative solutions. They will tend to see the differences between things (either/or dichotomies, analytical thinking). Help them see the relationships among things (both/and, wholistic thinking).

They will tend to be negative and independent in their thinking. Help them see the positive benefits of working together.

There are a number of Rebel Producer types.

1. **Deferrers.** Deferrers are dancers. They gracefully do the ol' sidestep. Deferrers avoid conflicts or uncomfortable situations by deferring to the law or to higher authority. They use the weight of the law to put off the other party without directly having to take a stand or say "no." It allows them to side-step being responsible and to sneak out of potentially troublesome situations. They take the superior posture of being the spokesperson for the social, moral, or legal conscience.

"I can't do that. It's against the law."
"Where would we be if everybody did that?"
"That's a heretical statement."
"I'm sorry, but that's against the company's policy."

In Response:

Refocus the discussion on the underlying issues. Confront and challenge. In the case of a conflict, point out that your issues are with them, not with higher authority. Confront them directly with their side-stepping and their avoidance of personal responsibility. Hold them accountable and point out the consequences for non-action. Explore with them what they need to be able to cooperate with you in directly addressing the problem or conflict instead of avoiding it.

For example:

"I'm not asking you to break the law. I'm asking you to honestly address the issues facing us and to work with me in solving them."

"I feel like I'm being put off. I'd like to address what's going on in our relationship. I'm wondering what you need to be willing to do that."

"I'm aware that my proposal might require a change or exemption from current policy. I believe current needs warrant such a change. By not allowing flextime, we are going to lose some of our most skilled employees. By using flextime, we can increase our productivity by 10 percent."

For example:

Store employee: You can't return items without a receipt.

Customer: I know your policy is not to accept returned goods without a receipt. However, I did buy this item here, it has your pricing label on it, and it is obviously defective. I appreciate your need to follow company policy. I need you to appreciate that I do not want to be cheated. I am not willing to leave here until I get my needs met.

Store employee: I don't have the authority to allow you to return it.

Customer: Then I'd like to speak to the person who does have the authority. I'm not leaving until I feel I have been fairly treated. I bought the item in good faith and I expect to be treated in the same manner.

Another example:

Nursery Owner: I'm calling because I have not received payment for invoice #123, and it is now two months overdue.

Garden Center Bookkeeper: "Our policy is to not pay from invoices. We have to receive a statement before I can issue a check.

Nursery Owner: I'm sure you have your own bookkeeping reasons for that policy. However, you did not state that policy on your purchase order. I resent the fact that you have gone for two months without paying your bill or stating your policy. The fact that you have not stated the policy makes me wonder if you use that as an excuse to delay paying your bills on time. I am not willing to be victimized by unstated policies. I'm not willing to be your banker. I want immediate payment of your overdue account.

G.C. Bookkeeper: I'm sorry you feel that way. I still have to have a statement before I can issue a check.

Nursery Owner: What happens if you pay a bill without a statement?

G.C.Bookkeeper: I must have a statement for our accountant.

Nursery Owner: I see. I'd like to suggest what I believe would be a fair agreement that would meet both our needs. Since you owe the bill and it is overdue, and since you did not inform me of your statement policy, and since you don't need to have the statement immediately but only for your records, would you agree to mail me a check today and I'll mail you a statement today? That way I'll get my check and you'll get your statement.

G. C. Bookkeeper: I suppose that would be OK. I'll send the check.

2. **Refusers.** Refusers are afraid of being trapped or judged or of somehow giving themselves away. They put others off by being above it all. They refuse to lower themselves by justifying their actions. Refusers have difficulty distinguishing between explaining themselves so others can understand their behavior and intentions and justifying themselves. They are afraid of being in a childlike position, asking for approval.

"I refuse to justify myself to you."
"I don't owe you any explanation."
"What I do is my choice."
"That's personal. I don't have to share it with you."

In Response:

First of all, try to avoid moving into a critical parent role. Try to melt them by explaining that you simply want to understand them, not control them. Point out the mutual benefits if you are better able to understand the intentions behind their behavior. If they don't melt, then confront them firmly, if you have some authority to do so. Again, it is important to explain why you need to know.

"I'm not asking you to justify yourself. I don't want to be your parent. I simply want to understand you."

"June, when you refuse to explain where you were, I am left with my own assumptions. Your refusal to explain makes me think you're trying to hide something. I end up feeling like I can't trust you and I feel uncomfortable giving you the car."

"What you do is your choice. At the same time, when your behavior affects me, it also becomes my business. I don't feel I can honestly recommend you for a raise when I am stuck with a project that is over budget without any explanation."

"I'm not asking you to share information about your personal life. I simply need a valid explanation of why you did not show up for work again today. Without an explanation I have no choice but to put you on probation."

3. **Dismissers.** Dismissers express their anger indirectly. They maintain their power and superior position by attempting to make the other person feel inferior, not wanted, in the way, not important, or not needed. They may send their message verbally or non-verbally. Non-verbally, they do it with a flip of their head or shoulder, with sarcasm, with superior silence, by turning their back, or by ignoring the other party.

"Get lost!"
"Nobody asked you."
"What do you know?"
"What are you doing here?"
"Who do you think you are?"

In Response:

Don't allow yourself to be intimidated. Remember that if they were not afraid of you, they would not have to dismiss you. Your first response should be to attempt to melt them by specifically and gently describing their behavior and letting them know how it affects you and what you would like to have from them. If they are still frozen, confront them more firmly and refuse to be dismissed. When you have their attention, invite them to do something more productive—such as refocusing on the real issues.

"When you walk away from me while I'm talking, I feel dismissed. I need to be understood and I'd like you to stay here and finish our conversation."

"I'm not willing to be ignored or to disappear into the woodwork. I do want to resolve the problems we have. Are you willing to do that with me?"

"I have more value than your behavior indicates. My temptation is to dismiss you in return, but I don't believe that will solve our problems. I want to refocus on the issues before us."

4. **Tough Guys/Gals.** These people are afraid of giving away their power and being dependent. They are afraid they can't

make it on their own, so they act tough and independent to prove to everyone (including themselves) that they do not need anyone. They are frequently sarcastic and explosive with their anger. They use their anger to bluff others and they are always testing their capabilities.

"I don't need you or anyone."
"If I need help, I'll ask for it."
"I don't need anything from you, Jimmy."

In Response:

The best response is to melt them. With a little warmth and humor, they usually drop their bravado. It also helps to reinforce them by letting them know you believe in their capability.

"You look like you could be fun if you weren't so tough."

"I believe you can do it yourself. My experience is that doing it all yourself is not the most fun—or the easiest way of getting something done."

"When you call me 'Jimmy,' I feel like a child who has just been dismissed by a parent. But I believe we both need some things from each other."

5. **Superior Types.** These people protect themselves by acting better than others. They walk and talk with their noses in the air. They maintain their superior position by being haughty and by making diminishing remarks that put others down. They make others feel dumb, less than, and not with it.

"You actually went there?"

"You're embarrassing. Personally, I wouldn't be caught dead driving one of those."

"Well, I suppose if that's all you can do, it's OK."

In Response:

The temptation is to always "one up" them or dismiss them in return. Instead, describe their behavior, let them know how it affects you, and invite them to not be superior. Nicely bring them down off the table and around to your side.

"Your comments make me feel like I'm stupid. I don't like being put down. I'm wondering what you would need to engage me on an equal level instead of acting superior."

"I feel like I've just been negated. What is it about me that you need to put me down? I don't want to play that game with you."

"I assume that if you really felt equal to me you wouldn't need to make me feel inferior. I'm wondering what I am doing to make you feel that way."

6. **Busy Bobs.** These people keep others away by not having time because they have so much to do. Being overly scheduled and committed allows them to feel more important, to avoid being responsible, and to avoid dealing with unpleasant issues. They keep themselves unavailable. They just never seem to have the time, or you can't catch them.

"I'm sorry, I don't have time right now."

"I wish I could, but I just have too much to do."

In Response:

Describe their behavior and ask them to explain their intentions. Confront them and point out consequences. Refuse to be put off and establish specific deadlines.

"I've called you every day for the past week to find out if my office is going to be finished on time. I assume you are trying to avoid me. I need to know if my assumptions are correct. I will have to pass on my costs to you for each day that we are delayed in moving."

"When will you have time? I want a definite answer."

"I'm not willing to be put off indefinitely. Until you clear up what happened, I won't authorize payment to you."

7. **Challengers.** Challengers push against. They push against authority figures and traditional ways. They don't care about titles or prestige. They want to know if you can do it. They don't care about promises. They want production. They don't care how it's been done in the past if they think they have a better way.

Challengers protect themselves by attempting to put the burden of proof on others. They take the offensive to make others feel intimidated and to make others justify themselves. They attempt to discredit credentials or positions.

"What are your credentials?"

"Just because that's how you've always done it doesn't mean I have to do it that way."

"You're going to have make a believer out of me."

"Show me. I don't believe it will work."

"Who are you?"

In Response:

Above all, don't push back. Draw them around to your side of the table. Try to move them from an either/or position to a both/and cooperative position. Let them know what you agree with and build on it instead of pitting yourself against them.

One option is to take the wind out of their offensive by asking them to explain what their motivation is for challenging you. Don't ask them why they are challenging you. To ask why will make them more defensive. Instead, attempt to focus on what the real issues are behind their challenge by inviting them to explain themselves and their needs.

A second option is to non-defensively explain to them whatever it is they are asking to have explained. Give them what they want and follow it up by asking what makes that explanation important for them or how they see it as contributing to solving the problem. Again, your intent is to focus on the underlying issues.

The importance of these approaches is that the other party's challenge may provide a valuable contribution to your negotiations. It may open up new options that you have failed to see. So, instead of becoming defensive and justifying yourself, treat their challenge as a constructive contribution to solving the problem. Make it work for you instead of against you.

"I've been a negotiator for fifteen years and have worked with a wide variety of organizations. I hear in your question your desire to find solutions for the current problem and your hope that I have the ability to successfully facilitate that process. What would make you more comfortable with my role in the process?"

"I agree that continuing to do something simply because that is how it was done in the past is not a good enough reason. Tell me more about your ideas and let's see if we can incorporate what seems to work from the past with your new ideas. Sounds like that might give us the best of both worlds."

"I'd like to make a believer out of you, but not in the sense of proving that I'm right and you're wrong. I'd like us both to believe that we can work together to reach a resolution."

"I'm aware that every time I suggest a solution, you argue with me about it. It feels as if you need to keep pitting us against each other. I'd like to build upon what you just said and see if we can find some mutual solutions. I'd like to focus on what we can agree on instead of continuing to focus on our differences."

Four Methods For Melting The Tough Rebels

1. Don't take them too seriously.
2. Melt them with warmth and humor.
3. Help them translate their either/or thinking into and/both thinking. Find your common ground instead of focusing on your differences. Refuse to get pitted against them.
4. Since they tend to be impatient and want immediate results, do your homework and give them just the nuts and bolts. If they want more than that, they'll let you know.

CHAPTER 11

GENERATOR PROFILE

Style of Thinking:	Dialectical. And/Both. Multi-Perspective. Sees through other's behavior.
Way of Relating:	Autonomous intimacy. Responsible to, not for. Trusting.
Core Needs:	Justice. Integration. Integrity. Creative solutions. Solving problems while maintaining relationships.
Key Emotions:	Confident strength. Balanced. Accepting. Feeling abundance and empathy.
Power:	Self-acceptance and trust.
Behavior:	Flexible. Listens. Takes others in. Sees through paradoxes. Focuses on values and needs rather than positions. Searches for mutual gain.
Beliefs:	In all my limitedness I am more than enough. People are not right or wrong. only different. The world is made up of a lot of little kids in adult bodies. I can trust myself and my experience.

Style of Negotiating: To understand and accept the real situation and search for mutually beneficial solutions.

CHAPTER 11

GENERATORS: GETTING MORE WITH LESS EFFORT

WHO IS A GENERATOR?

How do you know when you or others are thinking as a Generator?

Have you ever...

- Been involved in a negotiation and observed it at the same time?
- Confronted someone and had them listen to you and own responsibility for their own behavior?
- Been aware of being angry and wanting to punish someone and at the same time stayed in charge of your self and chose to negotiate a reasonable solution?
- Obtained someone's attention who was being aggressive toward you by drawing your boundaries without punishing or dismissing that person?
- Been able to see the scared kid inside a bully and felt compassionate and firm instead of angry and scared?
- Been able to perceive the multiple perceptions in a situation and been able to acknowledge the truth and value in each perception?
- Trusted yourself enough to choose to be vulnerable and not live up to others' worst fears of you?
- Been able to see through another's position to their underlying needs and interests?

- Taken others in without taking them on?
- Seen the truth in a paradox?
- Trusted that you could make it on your own and chosen to share the journey with others because it's more fun that way?
- Felt the satisfaction of healing an old pain in yourself?
- Felt the satisfaction of forgiving someone else or yourself?
- Felt the satisfaction of resolving a conflict with someone else?
- Persuaded someone to become reasonable and negotiate a resolution with you after he had been angry and defensive?
- Refused to play someone's manipulative game and invited her to do something more constructive instead?
- Felt patient and content?
- Negotiated a situation in which everyone walked away with enough of what they needed?
- Felt calm, self-trusting, and interested while listening to someone else's anger and criticism?

MEET A GENERATOR!

Generators are fully functioning adults who have learned to trust their own experience and perceptions. They have learned to listen to their actual feelings and needs and to take responsibility for getting what they want in direct ways. They have come to accept that, in their own limitedness, they are more than enough.

They are not nice guys or victims—they are simply more flexible and appropriate. They will cooperate with you as long as you cooperate with them because they believe that people can get more, produce better products, do it easier, and have more fun by cooperating.

However, as soon as you stop cooperating with them, as soon as you drop into lower levels of thinking and try to bully them or deceive them, they will be right in your face. They'll draw their boundaries and match your games. They'll do this not to punish you or cheat you, but because they are not willing to be victimized by you.

Not only will they confront your behavior, they will be better than you at negotiating because their thinking will be fully open. They'll see through your strategies, see the whole picture more realistically, weigh the relative merit of issues, and respond more effectively and flexibly. Instead of reacting, they will be acting on deliberate choices.

A single human brain functioning on a Generative level has informational processing capacities synonymous with AT&T. A person acting from Enforcer abilities has the capability of two tin cans and a string. Who do you think will win the negotiation? To negotiate from anything other than Generator capacities is to put yourself at a tremendous disadvantage.

Generator Scenarios

Imagine yourself as the chief executive officer of a hospital. With all the changes and increasing competition in the health-care field, your board and medical staff need to do cooperative long-range planning. You understand the pressures on your medical staff and why they feel resistant to cooperating in planning that will probably increase their financial limitations. You decide to have a planning retreat and to talk to the physicians individually to express your understanding and to emphasize strongly your need to have them participate.

Imagine yourself as an attorney representing a banking system. Because of poor investments, your client is about to be taken over by another banking corporation. The opposing attorneys are using public statements to embarrass your client and to lock him into conceding on some major points. You confront their senior negotiator, making it clear that you will not be forced to reach agreements through pressure. You insist on establishing fair criteria for the continuing negotiation process.

Imagine yourself as a manager. You need to confront a department head on his need to win and always be right when interfacing with other department heads. He has given excuses why he hasn't had time to meet with you. You walk into his office and tell him that while you know he's busy, you want to meet today and want him to name the time. He looks surprised and agrees to meet at eleven.

You run a small software company. A client calls who is enraged about the poor service your company has provided. Instead of justifying yourself or becoming defensive, you invite him to tell you more so you can understand what the problem is and how you can respond to it.

Imagine yourself as a therapist mediating with a divorcing couple over child-custody rights. They are feeling angry and defensive and keep making threats. Before talking with them about who will have what rights, you continually refocus them to talk about the values underlying what they want for their children and on fair procedures for sharing their parenting responsibilities.

Imagine yourself facilitating budget meetings. You've been assigned the task of reducing the budget by ten million dollars. As the tension builds in the group, you keep refocusing them on underlying principles and values. As someone challenges your objectivity, instead of getting angry or defensive, you ask him to explain what he needs.

As the personnel manager of your company, you are making a presentation to all of your managers on your organization's soon-to-be implemented performance review system. One of your managers continuously raises questions that challenge your proposal. Instead of justifying the proposal or debating with her, you build upon her comments and point out areas of common agreement. You refuse to get pitted against her.

Imagine your are a union negotiator sitting across the table from the management team. Past relationships have not been good, and you assume that once again the management team's primary goal is to break the union's power. The management team presents excessive demands, and you calmly ask them to explain how they arrived at those positions.

TRUSTING THAT YOU ARE ENOUGH

Qualitative differences exist between the first four and the fifth level of thinking. In the first four levels, persons negotiate from a posture of scarcity. They assume there will not be enough of whatever is being negotiated and they believe they must strategize to get their share. Persons operating from the first four levels assume other people will not be cooperative and therefore cannot be trusted. They are afraid they will not be clever and tough enough to negotiate effectively with the opposition.

On the first four levels, people operate from self-protective postures. They bully, make extreme demands, play games, try to please and obligate others, act superior and dismiss others. They resort to bargaining and compromising. They spend more energy protecting themselves than searching for creative solutions.

On the Generator level, negotiators function from a posture of reality-based abundance. While physical assets are limited, they believe they can get more than enough. They usually do. They understand the other person will often be operating on lower capacity levels and will therefore behave in self-protective ways. However, Generators believe they have the skills to move the other person into a cooperative posture and to reach a mutually satisfying solution.

Generators believe they are enough to take care of themselves. Generators face the facts and negotiate based on reality. Instead of wishing that other people were different, they realistically set about getting cooperation and weighing alternatives.

For example:

Sid had a rental house that he wanted to sell. His new renters had lived in the house for only two months, and during that time they had done some cosmetic damage. Sid needed to get them out so he could clean up the house and put it on the market.

When he called to inform them that he wanted them to move, his renters became angry and refused. At this point, Sid had several options. He could decide not to sell; to sell it with them in it; to legally force them out (at the cost of three months and some expense while they did more damage to the house); or to work it out so both sides were satisfied. He decided on the last option.

The renters were angry about the inconvenience of having to move again so soon. Furthermore, they did not have the money to make a deposit on another house. Sid agreed to refund their cleaning and damage deposit if they agreed to move by the end of the month. He apologized for the inconvenience, offered to help them find another place, and even offered to help them move. The renters felt satisfied and moved by the end of the month, and Sid did not have to help them move. Both sides parted on friendly terms.

Because they trust themselves enough, Generators do not have to make a big killing from every situation out of a fear that they won't be able to get enough tomorrow. Instead, Generators characteristically need (among other things):

- To arrive at just and equitable solutions.
- To have ongoing, satisfying relationships.
- To live with what is—the reality that both sides have needs.
- To be congruent—to be who they say they are.
- To be simultaneously autonomous and intimate—to be involved and in real contact without losing themselves in the process.
- To be creative.

Given these needs, familiar emotions for Generators include:

Acceptance	*Expansiveness*
Trust	*Compassion*
Confidence	*Warmth*
Gentleness and strength	*Peacefulness*
Gratefulness	*Anticipation*
Excitement	*Interest*
Empathy	*Clarity*
Firmness	*Generosity*

SEEING THE BIG PICTURE

A primary advantage in negotiating on a Generative level is the number of options available to you for getting what you want from others. Enforcers only have one option–FORCE. If Force doesn't work, they then must withdraw out of fear. Scorekeepers can do what Enforcers do, plus they can use their grab bag of games and strategies. Peacemakers can do what Enforcers and Scorekeepers do plus they can make others feel guilty and obligated–and so on up the line.

Only Generators have all options available to use. Only Generators are free to choose the response that will be most appropriate to the given situation. The reason for this is because Generator thinking is both dialectical and wholistic. Generators are capable of "both/and" rather than "either/or" thinking. Generators can simultaneously understand multiple perspectives on multiple levels. As a Generator, you can:

- See the entire picture.
- Appreciate the relevance and value of each person's perspective.
- See the relationship between multiple perspectives and weigh their relative merits.
- Assess complex, casual relationships in solving problems.
- See through structures and behavior to understand underlying principles, values, and needs.
- Be conscious of what is going on in yourself, in others, in your relationship, in the process, and in the content of the discussion–all at the same time.

Simultaneously, you have the complex, analytical ability to break problems into their components, to separate the problem issues, the relationship issues, and the process issues from each other. You have the flexibility to quickly shift your focus and address each of these issues as needed. In this way you will be simultaneously diffused and focused in your thinking. You will be able to step back and take a look at what's happening and to be present to the negotiation all in the same moment. You will stay focused on the problem while removing relationship blocks and attending to the obvious.

For example:

David is on the steering committee for the merger of two local hospitals, St. Elizabeth's and Memorial. The problem before the committee is to decide whether one or both hospitals will continue to provide in-patient surgery.

During the past hour, several issues have been raised: the cost savings of locating all surgical procedures at Memorial; whether patients would travel across town to Memorial or go to other hospitals in the nearby metropolitan area; the effect on other departments at St. Elizabeth's if the surgical ward is closed; the resistance on the part of St. Elizabeth's medical staff; the public image impact on St. Elizabeth's; and the possibility of creating an out-patient, day surgery unit at St. Elizabeth's.

David is thinking about all of these issues and weighing the importance of various comments. He is deciding which of these issues is most significant, i.e., if they are not resolved, they could block the proposed merger. He believes the issues fall into three categories: financial considerations, quality of service, and impact on people.

David is aware of the group's rising tension. The medical staff representative is angrily calling those in favor of the move stupid and naive. David understands that the medical staff potentially has the most to lose by the merger and that the doctors are frightened.

David realizes that the group needs to shift its focus from the problem (where to locate surgical services) to what's happening inside each member and between all the members. He suggests they take a five-minute break, then come back to share their fears and concerns. The group agrees.

In the example, we see David using the type of multiple-perspective thinking that is characteristic of Generators. At the same time that he is aware of each side's behavior and underlying needs (seeing through), he is also using his analytical abilities to break the problem into its components (three categories of issues). He is separating the different categories of issues and focusing on what the next step in the process needs to be (take a break and focus on the underlying needs). He is able to separate the problem (where to locate in-patient surgery) from what is going on internally. And he is willing to address the relationship conflicts that are developing.

As Generators, we realize that there is no single right solution to a problem. Instead, there are multiple solutions, each of which carries its own consequences. Therefore, we play at creatively expanding our options instead of narrowing them. We "brainstorm" and evaluate the relative value of all our options.

In the example above, instead of hooking into an either/or argument, or a who-has-the-right-solution fight, David helps the group cool down (and therefore expand their styles of thinking) by taking a break. This allows them to have a better chance at refocusing on understanding and accepting all the factors in the problem so they can get on the same team and cooperatively create solutions that will meet more of their needs.

In Generative thinking, we are better able to see through paradoxes and to perceive the unity in polarities. We are able to see what we have in common with others as well as what separates us.

For example:

Charlie is a grape grower in the valley. The grape harvesting season is only a few weeks long. Therefore, timing in moving his grapes to the market is major factor in the price he can get. If he can hit the market early, before the glut, he can get a better price.

From an Enforcer or Scorekeeper perspective, it makes sense for Charlie to pick his grapes while they are still green and beat the other growers to the market. While this may be to Charlie's short-term advantage (he'll make more profit this year), it is not to his long-term advantage.

The price the growers from a particular region receive depends upon the quality of their product and the region's reputation. The quality of grapes depends upon their sugar content, which means they need to be picked when ripe. If all the growers from the region pushed green grapes onto the market, the price the region will get in the marketplace will drop.

From a Generator perspective, Charlie must make a long-term decision. Instead of pushing for the big kill this year, he might get the growers to agree when to pick so that by cooperating they can all be more profitable over the long term.

Does this mean Charlie is a nice guy? No. He's just smart enough to see through an apparent paradox: by cooperating and not being greedy, he can be more profitable (in the long run).

Another example:

Joel manages the loading dock for a fresh produce packer. Near the end of the season, when only a few trucks come in, it is not cost effective to keep the dock open eight hours a day. In addition, Joel's salary is based in part on incentives–how low he can keep overhead costs. It is more profitable for him personally, and to the company in the short-term, to close the dock. But the growers, especially in a bad year, want to get all the produce they can to market. They want the dock open. And the company's sales manager, Lorraine, also wants the dock open so she and her staff can make more commissions.

Joel and Lorraine discuss the problem with the plant manager. Approaching it from a Generative perspective, they do not get into blaming or criticizing, complaining or bargaining. Instead, they work together to understand all the needs of the various parties. They keep the problem out there as a mutual issue rather than getting defensive and polarized. They search for a way to meet everyone's needs.

The solution? They determine that, given volume, it would be cost-effective and profitable to keep the dock open three hours a day. Lorraine agrees to canvas the growers daily to find out who plans to ship produce the next day and to let them know the hours the dock is open.

The results? Joel doesn't lose any incentive salary. The company, the sales staff, and the grower make more money. The company has also made a good public relations move. And finally, the growers feel that the packing company is looking out for the growers' interests. Everybody wins!

Expanding Your Options

We are able to achieve these kinds of results as Generators because we operate from multiple perspective thinking.

Focusing on the underlying needs of all parties involved leads us to see more options. Seeing more options allows us to feel more capable and powerful. As a result of our integrated thinking, we operate from beliefs based on self-trust and on a more realistic trust of others.

As Generators we realize:

- Everyone has a piece of the truth.
- I can trust my own perceptions and feelings.
- I can get what I want.
- People are not bad, lazy or selfish, just more or less afraid of not getting what they need.
- I will know what to do when the time comes.
- I have value and worth, and so do others.
- I can achieve what I want.
- It's OK to discover and risk.
- I'm good for me.
- Life is abundant.
- Life has meaning and purpose.
- Everyone does their best most of the time.
- It's safe to let go and see what happens.
- I can afford to listen to others and understand them.
- My greatest strength lies in trusting myself and not having to hide.
- Facing reality is easier than running away from it.
- I can be angry without losing control.
- The anger of others will not destroy me.
- There are many valid solutions to every problem.
- Conflicts can be resolved.

Reflected in all of these beliefs are acceptance and self-trust. As Generators we believe we are enough to face reality directly. As a result, we see more and hear more and in the process create more options for getting others to do what we want them to do. We are more conscious.

GETTING OTHERS TO WANT TO COOPERATE

On this level, relationships take on a new dimension. As Generators, we are able to "take others in" without "taking them on" or losing ourselves in the process. We are clear about our own boundaries and do not give ourselves away.

As a Generator, I can be aware that you will be uncomfortable if I confront you honestly about your poor performance, but I don't use your possible discomfort as an excuse for not confronting you when I need to do so. I can appreciate the fact that you need to be independent and do things your own way, but as your supervisor, I won't allow you to be independent to the detriment of the team.

As Generators, we have the empathetic capacity to understand others on multiple levels. We are not naive. We realize that others are often defensive and non-productive or destructive. At the same time, we believe that people are not right or wrong, good or bad—they are simply scared. In the earlier example, David was not intimidated by the physicians' fear, and he redirected the meeting to respond to those fears instead of avoiding them.

For example:

Recently, I was in the office of a friend who is a commercial real estate broker, when one of his clients, the developer of large retail complexes, came storming in. The verbal assault, which isn't printable here, boiled down to a series of accusations against my friend's sales staff.

The developer had made it big during the 1970s—mainly by being lucky enough to be in the right place at the right time. Now, mortgaged up to his armpits in a glutted market, he was afraid of losing it all. My friend had been able to lease only 40 percent of the developer's space. Although this was above the local market average, the developer blamed the sales staff for being lazy, ineffectual, and disinterested.

My friend was able to calm the developer down by getting his attention ("Harry, shut up and listen to me for a minute"), and by explaining to Harry what they were doing with their marketing plan. Harry felt reassured and agreed to cooperate with the sales staff by not calling them and cussing them out five times a day.

As Generators, we realize that inside the adults we deal with are little kids who are doing the best they know how to do. We believe that when people know how to do things better, they do. We believe that when people are not scared, they begin to act in more cooperative and productive ways.

Thus, instead of reacting, we act in appropriate ways that get the other party's attention and cooperation. We get tough when we need to and take the other person in when that is needed.

More Than Enough Power–Key Characteristics

1. As Generators, we are able to create safe environments for others because we feel safe with ourselves. We choose to be appropriately vulnerable. We can afford to take risks and be transparent so others can see us as real flesh and blood people like themselves. In doing this, we make it safe for others to risk being honest and open.

For example:

If as my sales manager you want me to sell our product your way and I can't do that, I'll tell you that I feel anxious and overwhelmed and trapped instead of agreeing to do what you want and then going off and doing nothing. If I'm feeling stuck because I don't have an answer to your question, I'll let you know that and invite you to join me in searching for an answer.

2. As Generators, we make it easy for others to understand us instead of expecting others to read our minds. We are aware how often we tell others what we want them to do and expect them to intuit why we want it done and how important it is to us. It's one thing to tell a secretary to do a job. It's another matter to explain to her why it is important.
3. As Generators, we actively listen to others instead of planning our defense while the other person is talking. We are able to listen on multiple levels at the same time. We can hear the other person's content or words while also being aware of the voice tone, the nonverbal messages, and the speaker's emotions. In

doing this, we hear the whole message more accurately.

You can tell me to do a task my own way. What those words really mean depends upon your tone of voice. You may mean it (congruent voice tone) or you may not (sarcastic voice).

4. As Generators, we know that power does not rest simply in how big someone is or how clever or tough they are. Nor does power reside in socially sanctioned authority. Power resides within ourselves.

As generators, we believe that in our own limitedness we are more than enough. We trust our own experience and perceptions and emotions and skills. We believe that whatever arises, we will be able to respond appropriately. Instead of avoiding, we confront. Instead of planning our defense, we listen.

As Generators, we trust our own truth and our own strength. We surprise others by not living up to their worst fears.

For example:

- The other person expects that you will ignore the conflict and not bring it up, but you bring it up. You say what you are feeling and needing.
- The other person expects you to deny responsibility for your part in the problem, but you acknowledge what you see that you did wrong.
- They expect you to come out fighting, but you ask them instead in a quiet voice what they are thinking about and what they want from you. And you feed back what you hear them saying instead of justifying your position.

5. We understand the difference between attacking out of rage and being in charge of our anger enough to explain what it is about and what we want from the other person. We understand there is a difference between being overreactive and drawing definitive and firm boundaries.

As generators, we are not victims. We are gentle lions and lionesses. Our strength is quiet, deriving from our self-trust and self-confidence.

6. As a result, Generators can afford to understand others, to take others in, and to appreciate the truth in

other's perceptions. Generators do not have to make others wrong or bad in order to justify themselves or to be right. They invite others' anger and criticism so that they can understand the whole situation and take responsibility for their own part.

7. The primary objective of a Generator is to arrive at what is true and just. Their basic posture in the world is: in order to get what they need from others, they need only to trust themselves and to understand and acknowledge the value and limitations of others. *Generators believe that if they face what is and work with it, they can always get more than enough.* That doesn't mean they will always get what they want, when they want it, from whom they want it—but they will always get more than enough.

Gentle Lions and Lionnesses

Characteristic behaviors of Generators from their posture of self-confidence include:

Using consensus decision-making
Using gentle, firm strength
Being empathetic
Acting from self-appropriated values
Inviting rather than persuading
Planning appropriately
Being transparent
Taking others in
Being in charge
Confronting firmly without dismissing
Being patient
Being accepting
Initiating
Being flexible
Being generous
Being honest
Listening actively
Being a mentor
Being interdependent

Implications For Negotiating From A Generative Stance: Don't Settle For Less

If you are not negotiating from Generative capacities, you are cheating yourself. You are working harder than you need to work. You are losing more than you need to lose. You are creating scarcity when you could have abundance. You are settling for less.

Your objective in negotiating is to get yourself and the other person onto a Generative level long enough to reach a resolution. This is important for three key reasons:

1. Only on this level can both persons see the whole situation and accurately evaluate the elements to solve the problems and move toward resolution.
2. Only on this level can conflicts be resolved. Problems can be solved more or less effectively at each of the lower levels, but relationship conflicts cannot. Only in Generative thinking can you achieve the total objective of getting what you want from others while maintaining satisfying relationships.
3. Settlements and solutions agreed upon on a Generator level are more likely to be kept and honored. Agreements reached on a Generator level are clean agreements. They do not have unfinished business associated with them. They are consensual agreements to which all parties are cognitively and emotionally committed.

In lower stage agreements, one or both parties will walk away feeling they have been forced, conned, obligated, or dismissed, that they have compromised and settled for less than they wanted. Consequently, they walk away with some degree of resentment and either will not fully implement the agreement or sabotage it. Generative agreements, on the other hand, may need to be renegotiated as circumstances or conditions change, but this will be done up-front in a direct and honest manner.

Other good reasons to negotiate as a Generator:

1. Because of their capacities for multiple-perspective thinking, Generators are more skilled at accurately analyzing, evaluating, and solving problems. They are more conscious and therefore more reality-based.
2. They are capable of generating more creative solutions because they don't get limited by looking for or defending the "right" answer.

3. Generators see through behavior and positions and are able to refocus the negotiation on underlying needs and interests. Hence, Generators do not get forced or hustled into unsatisfactory solutions and are able to keep negotiations moving.
4. Generators are capable of functioning from multiple levels at the same time. Consequently, they have all the behavioral options available to them in a negotiating situation.
5. Generators are able to be actively involved in a negotiation and at the same time aware of their relationship with the other person. Thus they can negotiate the problem and the relationship simultaneously and make appropriate decisions about when to shift their focus to one or the other.

In response to the other person's personal attacks, part of a Generator may feel like attacking back, while another part will recognize that attacking back would be counterproductive. The Generator will understand that the other person is attacking because he feels threatened. Generators will recognize the fear behind the aggressive behavior and employ one or more options: refocus on the issues; calmly call attention to the behavior to take the wind out of it; invite the other person to explore more productive options; assertively draw a boundary to get the other person's attention.

Not only can they negotiate the problem and the relationships, they are also aware of the process (how we are negotiating), and the criteria (standards for settlement).

6. Generators are aware of their own internal dialogue and emotions. They are able to be consciously aware of their self-protective beliefs and behaviors. Therefore, they can choose not to be limited by them. As a result, Generators do not give their power away.

For example:

I may feel like withdrawing and punishing you silently, but I will decide that won't get either of us what we want in the long run. Or, I may be tempted to concede and say "Yes" when I want to say "No," but I'll say "No" and explain what my needs are.

7. Because they trust themselves, Generators are able to be more flexible and adaptive. They can afford to be vulnerable, which invites the other person to be the same. Generators can understand others without having to "beat" them.

For example:

We own a business together and have decided that I am going to buy you out. Instead of going into the negotiation with the firm position that I will not give you more than $200,000, I will focus my pre-discussion planning on getting clear about what I need short-term and long-term—in terms of cash flow, indebtedness, freedom to run the business my own way, an ongoing relationship with you, etc. In the actual negotiations, I will focus the discussion on understanding your needs (immediate cash for another venture, guaranteed long-term income, etc.) and on letting you know what I need. I will trust that by understanding and accepting your needs and by explaining as fully as possible my needs, we will reach a creative settlement that will allow us both to leave satisfied with the relationship intact.

8. Generators actively listen and hear whole messages. Thus, they can more accurately identify the other person's needs and respond more appropriately. They are able to create safe environments which enable everyone to expand his or her capacities and be more cooperative.

Conclusion of Section 2

Developmental theory has many implications for effectively negotiating with others. Understanding development is imperative for understanding behavior. For instance, quietness can mean many different things depending upon the intentions behind the behavior. Being quiet can mean the other person is:

- Withdrawing out of fear to protect herself. (Enforcer)

- Pouting as a strategy to get what he wants. (Scorekeeper)
- Trying not to look foolish in the eyes of others. (Peacemaker)
- Dismissing others and feeling superior. (Rebel Producer)
- Feeling self-confident and assessing her most appropriate response. (Generator)

The intentionality behind the behavior is determined by the thinking level of the individual at the time the behavior is occurring. To accurately understand the message, meaning, or motivation behind behavior, it is important to be able to recognize the level on which the individual is thinking.

The same behavior can come from any one of the five levels. To be able to appropriately and effectively respond to others in a negotiation, it is important to be able to identify their current level or stage of thinking.

At the same time, certain behaviors and beliefs are characteristic of different levels. In fact, certain behaviors and perceptions are possible only at certain levels. Enforcers, for example, cannot perceive when they are being irrational and cannot understand the intentions behind behavior. They are not able to appreciate the effect their behavior is having on others.

In the midst of a negotiation, Enforcers are behaviorally limited to using aggression (demanding, attacking, pushing, forcing, threatening, controlling), or to physically and/or emotionally running away out of fear. It is not a question of being intentionally stubborn, abusive, or uncooperative. This is all that they are presently capable of being. Generators, on the other hand, have the whole range of perceptual and behavioral options available to them.

Understanding the limitations that thinking levels place on an individual's options enables us to realistically understand and accept what we are up against, and what we need to do to move the negotiations to a successful resolution. *Being able to recognize the capacity limitations or thinking level of the other person gives us important information about how to appropriately respond to get desired results.*

For example:

If we judge that an individual is being obstinate and intentionally refusing to acknowledge our needs, we may become angry and aggressive in return. But, the result if this person is an Enforcer will be a further constriction of his capacities, causing him to be more entrenched and uncooperative. On the other hand, if we recognize that he is threatened and is functioning from the height of his current capacities, we will look for some way to get his attention and help him feel safer. We may do this by slowing down the pace of the discussion, by actively listening so he feels understood, or by giving him some time to calm down. If we can help him feel safer, his capacities will expand and we will have a better chance of achieving a mutually beneficial resolution.

This same principle is true for all the other levels. By recognizing and accepting the other person's thinking level, we will be able to respond in ways that expand their capacities and enable them to cooperate.

Remember:

1. Human beings function out of different levels of thinking and relating. These levels are developmental and progress from simple to more complex.
2. Persons at each level perceive and experience the world differently and therefore have a certain range of behavioral responses available to them. As you move through the levels, you have more behavioral options for negotiating available to you.
3. Capacity levels do not remain constant. Throughout a given negotiation, individuals will move in and out of the various levels, depending upon how safe or threatened they feel.
4. Depending on their level, individuals negotiate differently. It is to your advantage to negotiate on a Generator level and create an environment safe enough so the other person can do the same.
5. At each level, power is understood differently. Your greatest power derives from trusting yourself and choosing to be appropriately vulnerable.

6. Problems can be solved more or less effectively from any of the levels, but conflicts (relationship breakdowns) can be resolved only on the Generator level. It is only at this level that you will be able to take others in and understand them without feeling you must defensively protect yourself.

SECTION III

THE FOUR CORE PRINCIPLES OF NO-FAULT NEGOTIATING

Every theory must have its underlying principles. No-Fault Negotiating is no exception.

The principles presented in this section are cornerstones for the No-Fault negotiating process. They provide a foundation for analyzing a negotiating situation—for identifying the key issues which must be brought into focus and addressed. As such, the principles are also a tool for planning and for implementing our plans—for understanding what is going on, for deciding what we can do about it, and for getting what we want from others.

The four founding principles are:

- *Create a Safe Environment.*
- *Shift Your Focus.*
- *Understand Others, Don't Beat Them.*
- *Attend to the Obvious.*

Taken together, these four principles are a synthesis of applying the developmental theory we have presented. Using these four principles will get you more of what you need, more often. They will enable you to create a cooperative climate in which both parties negotiate from Generative thinking. If you want to know how to keep yourself in Generative thinking, these principles are the answer.

CHAPTER 12

PRINCIPLE #1: CREATE A SAFE ENVIRONMENT

TAKING DEFENSIVENESS OUT OF YOUR NEGOTIATIONS

Contrary to popular belief and common practice, in most cases it is to our advantage:

- Not to intimidate the other person.
- Not box the opposition into the corner.
- Not put the opposition off balance.
- Not see how difficult we can make it for them.

Our job in a negotiation is to see how easy we can make it for others to cooperate with us.

When we understand the developmental process in human beings, we see that people function on different levels. Further, our ability to think and to relate to others fluctuates. The more stressed, pressured, or threatened we feel, the more our capacities constrict. The safer and more relaxed we feel, the more our capacities expand. Highly threatened adults function as Enforcers. As they feel safer and their capacities expand, they increasingly acquire more options. Adults who feel very safe and secure in themselves function as Generators.

This principle has important consequences for negotiating. The more expanded our capacities are, the better able we are to perceive the complexity of a situation. When we are functioning on the Generator level, we also are able also to weigh the relative importance of related factors. Thus, on a Generator level we are better able to distinguish between symptoms and core issues needing to be addressed.

We know that it makes no sense to talk about inventory control or our revenue budget when the real issue is the ongoing conflict in our relationship. We know it is pointless to keep pressing you for a commitment when you are playing "Yes, but" to our proposals. Instead, we will explore what your resistance is about. We won't push you to make the sales call our way. Instead, we'll search for mutual agreement about the client and her needs, what our goals are, and finally how we think the sales call can accomplish our goals.

Reflecting Mirrors: Do As I Do

In Generative thinking, we can be aware of multiple factors simultaneously. All at the same time, we can understand:

1. The Content—what it is we are taking about.
2. The Scope—both the bigger picture and the more detailed focus.
3. The Relationship—the level of understanding and acceptance between ourselves and the other party.
4. The Underlying Needs or Values—in the other person as well as in ourselves.
5. The Process—how we are negotiating with each other.
6. The Criteria—the criteria or standards each of us are using for negotiating a just settlement.

We can only do all this in Generative thinking. But, while it is crucial that we function from Generative capacities, it is equally important that we create an environment which invites the other person to do the same. The most effective way to do this is for us to negotiate from a Generative stance.

Human beings function as mirrors. We push against others and they push back. We bargain with others and they bargain back. If we approach others from a Generative posture of understanding and mutual problem-solving, they will be most likely to respond in kind.

When we find the other person is uncooperative, that tells us they are not feeling safe. Our task in negotiating is to help others feel safer so their capacities expand. In practice, however, we often do the opposite. We have falsely assumed that it was to our advantage to put the "opposition" at a disadvantage—to intimidate them, to make them feel less powerful. Or, as a recent seminar participant remarked, "That's crazy. Why would I want to give them any advantage?"

Our self-protective tendency is to figure out how to arrange the environment to have the upper hand. We carefully select the color of our clothing to make sure it communicates power. We try to get the other person to meet on our turf so we feel comfortable and more in control. We find out all we can about the other person so we know their vulnerable points. We act tough and dismissing to intimidate them. We plan our strategies to take their power away.

What we end up with is resistance, defensiveness, lack of trust, competitiveness, and counter-strategies aimed at making us powerless. Much of the literature on negotiating is written with this intent. It is aimed at instructing readers on how to be competitive bargainers rather that negotiators.

Competitive Bargaining Versus Negotiating

Competitive bargaining and negotiating are two different processes. Each is based on different assumptions. Each has different objectives. Competitive bargaining is based on the assumption that people cannot be trusted and are out to get all they can at everyone else's expense. The objective, therefore, is to "get" the other person before he or she "gets" us.

No-fault negotiating, on the other hand, is based on the assumption that people will usually respond in trustworthy ways when they are treated in trustworthy ways—*that people only become self-protective and grabby when they assume someone is trying to take advantage of them and they feel cheated or wary*. The objective in no-fault negotiating is to create a safe environment in which both parties do not have to become self-protective and can therefore afford to trust each other enough to work toward a mutually beneficial solution.

This is not a "Pollyanna" fantasy about human beings. And it does not mean that everyone is trustworthy. Many people are walking around with a lot of old, unhealed pain and with past experiences that make them operate from lower levels of thinking, from self-protective behaviors. Sometimes it is not easy to get their attention and convince them.

For example:

I recently interviewed the chief financial officer of a corporation who had been burned by a previous consultant. This consultant betrayed his confidence by sharing confidential information with the president of the corporation. It took several meetings before this particular person was willing to share real data. I had to earn his trust.

Human beings can become trustworthy and cooperative if the proper climate is created. Even if they have learned to protect themselves by being abusive or scheming most of the time, they are also capable of being open and straightforward.

It is tempting to get drawn down to another person's level. If they are being intimidating, our first impulse will be to respond with intimidation or to withdraw out of fear. If they are judging our competence, the temptation will be to judge them in return or to justify ourselves. It is very easy to be drawn into a blame game or scorekeeping, but that simply makes the situation worse.

When someone accuses us of not listening, our usual response is: "You're not listening to me either!" Both persons become more rigid and dig in to protect themselves. The result: our negotiations get stuck. We don't go anywhere. When we find the other person being defensive and operating from lower stage capacities, we need to make congruent personal contact with them. Real contact. Like a laser beam, we need to cut through their protective shield. We need to melt their crusty exterior. We need to say, "I believe we are probably both guilty of not listening. What do you need for me to understand?"

THE THREE SOURCES OF DEFENSIVENESS

We will eliminate defensiveness more often if we focus on what is threatening the other person. Usually what is threatening them will originate from one or more of three sources: environmental factors, their personal beliefs and perceptions, and what we are doing behaviorally.

1. ENVIRONMENTAL FACTORS

Environmental factors are current external conditions that affect a person's capacities for thinking. Environmental factors are whatever else is going on in the other person's life that may be influencing or pressing him. These conditions are often not a part of the immediate situation, but they affect the other person's perceptions, interests, needs, and behavior.

The time of day, the day of the week, the weather, the economy, what is happening in their organization, who their supervisor is, what is happening in their personal life, their age or gender, what their past experience has been, and which side of the bed they got up on—these are all potential environmental factors. If the other person's kid was just arrested for drug possession, or if he is under the gun from his boss and needs to prove himself, his capacities are probably not up to normal. As a result, he may be more anxious and less able to listen to other points of view. He may come across as defensive or demanding or unnecessarily accommodating.

Send 'em Home A Hero

When considering the environmental factors affecting the other person, we need to consider to whom they need to look good. Everyone has a constituency. Everyone has someone or a group of someones whose opinions of them are important. Everyone worries about what some people think of them.

From a practical perspective, we want to help the other person go home looking like a hero. We need to see whether we are asking them to agree to something or to do something that we would be unwilling to do. If we can't reach a settlement that allows them to feel successful and unembarrassed, then we are probably not going to get the cooperation we want from them.

In dealing with a union bargaining team, we can't expect them to cooperate with us if they have to take back a proposal that will get them booed out of the hall. If the terms of the proposal are essential to meet the needs of the company, then at the very least we need to help them plan how they can present the proposal, perhaps by giving them adequate supporting data. The same would be true if the management bargaining team had to take back an unpopular proposal.

How To Use Their Constituency For Your Advantage

Again, the objective is not to beat them. At the same time, the other person's constituency can also be used as leverage against them when we need to get their attention.

For example:

A restaurant located less than a block away applied for waiver of the city's liquor ordinance so they could build a bar in the restaurant. The city council quickly and quietly approved the waiver.

In planning their response to the city council, the board members of the school did a little homework on the constituencies of each city council member. The board learned that the owners of the restaurant had been major backers of three of the council members—three of the four who voted in favor of the restaurant.

The school board set up a meeting with those council members and presented them with their data. The board requested that the city council reconsider the waiver in an open meeting or they would be forced to release their information to the news media. No public hearing was held, but the waiver was reconsidered in light of new information—and denied.

In this instance, the school got what it wanted because it did its homework. The board considered the environmental factors and how to use those factors as leverage. The board was also willing to draw its boundaries, to get the other party's attention by pointing out the consequences of non-action. It worked!

As this example illustrates, environmental factors provide us with important information. These factors can tell us who has the power to make decisions and what will influence those decisions. The environmental factors also give us important information about timing and strategy. They can tell us what the other person needs and when and how to approach him.

Don't Make Excuses

Environmental factors, however, are never the primary issue. They are never the substance of the negotiation. They are merely a source of information. We want to use them in our negotiations, not use them for an excuse.

We don't want to use environmental factors as an excuse to avoid doing what we need to do. Even if the other person has financial problems or is going through a divorce or already has too much to do, we must still confront him.

Out of our own fear of confronting, we are sometimes tempted to sidestep the real issues. Environmental factors frequently give us the out we wanted. Before deciding to let the matter pass, consider the price you have to pay. Are you setting up your own worst expectations? If you don't confront the issue, what is most likely to happen?

2. The Other Person's Beliefs and Perceptions

The second source of defensiveness in a negotiation is what people bring to this situation from their past experience. Their beliefs and assumptions affect how they interpret present events.

For example:

Douglas owns a property-management firm. One of his clients is a psychologist who owns a conference center. The psychologist uses the conference center for his own seminars and has Douglas rent it out when he isn't using it for himself.

Douglas made a mistake and double-booked the center. The mistake caused several problems for the psychologist, including an expensive lawsuit for breach of contract. He wanted Douglas to be responsible for his mistake and to pay part of the losses.

When the psychologist confronted him about the matter, Douglas immediately became defensive. He had grown up in a family in which he felt unfairly blamed and was not given a fair hearing. As an adult, he believed other people would unreasonably blame him and would not listen to him.

Douglas had learned to protect himself by trying to be perfect and by hiding any mistakes he made. When those behaviors didn't work and he was confronted, he would either try to shift the responsibility to someone else or try to get sympathy by becoming a helpless martyr. "I did everything I could. I don't know what more I could have done. As hard as I try, I end up getting blamed for everything."

In this case, the psychologist refused to buy into the martyr game. He described to Douglas the facts of what had occurred and his martyred behavior. He explained how the situation was affecting him, what he needed, and what he wanted Douglas to do so they could maintain an ongoing relationship of mutual trust. Douglas backed off from his martyr position, agreed to pay for part of the losses, and is still managing the conference center.

The point is that other people's defensiveness may not be a result of present circumstances or anything we are doing. Their defensiveness may be a result of their childhood experiences, or of previous failures, or painful times as adults.

A person who grew up as the oldest child in a family, always had to take responsibility for younger siblings, and had to do more than her share may become resentful and resistive when her boss asks her to take on additional responsibilities. The person whose father always had a better idea or the "right" answer may become argumentative whenever someone else states a slightly different opinion. The person who was laid off after devoting twenty years of her life to a company may balk when her new supervisor talks about loyalty to the company.

Don't Pay The Price

In a negotiation, we are not responsible for the other person's past experiences and subsequent beliefs. It is not our responsibility to make up for what happened to them in the past. We don't deserve to be punished or to pay a price for what others have done to them.

For example:

As an auditor for the Department of the Interior, Jody traveled around the country doing audit reports at federally-owned sites. She had taken over the territory of a previous auditor whose style was pushy, sarcastic, and demeaning. The result was that she encountered automatic resistance and sometimes outright defiance from the site managers. They assumed she would treat them as her predecessor had.

In this instance, as in the example of the psychologist, Jody didn't deserve the response she was receiving from the site managers. Neither the immediate circumstances nor her behavior was creating the resistance and defensiveness. She was not responsible for what had happened in the past.

At the same time, the site manager's resistance was her present reality—that's what she had to deal with. Their resistance presented a problem. She had the choice of getting hooked into Level Two Scorekeeper capacities or accepting the real situation and confronting it from a Generator posture. Fortunately, she chose to do the latter.

Jody described to her clients what was happening, empathized with their past experience, let them know how it was affecting her, and assured them it was not her intent to make them look bad. Instead, she wanted to have cooperative relationships in which she could work with them to assess their management practices and help them find ways to do their jobs more easily and effectively.

Jody was successful in developing cooperative relationships with all the site managers. In turn, she was able to do her work more quickly and effectively than her predecessor. Her success was the result of her ability to create a safe environment.

Rather than getting hooked into lower level defensiveness, Jody managed to stay on a Generative level. She accepted the needs of her clients without taking responsibility for them. She confronted their behavior and invited them to relate to her in more productive ways.

Four Ways To Get Their Cooperation

When the other person is uncooperative because of her past experiences:

1. Clarify for yourself whether this defensiveness is the result of current or past events.

   If the sources of the other person's behaviors are in the past and did not involve you, you are not responsible for the past.

2. At the same time, acknowledge that the other person's defensiveness is your present reality, even if you didn't cause it.
3. Avoid dropping into lower levels. Don't respond to an attack with a counter-attack. Don't get into a blame game and don't become an avoiding Peacemaker.
4. Stay with Generative capacities. Confront the other person's behavior and let him know what you need. Invite him to relate to you in more productive ways. If he doesn't want to play fair, get his attention and draw your boundaries, as the psychologist did with Douglas. Then invite him to relate more productively.

3. Our Own Behaviors: Four Patterns That Reduce Defensiveness

The third cause of defensiveness in the other person is our own self-protective behavior. People mirror our thinking levels and behavior. If we blame them, they will usually blame us in response. Then we are stuck in a Scorekeeper standoff. If we dismiss them, they will usually dismiss us. Then we get stuck in a Rebel Producer standoff.

All of our lower level, self-protective behaviors produce defensiveness in others:

- Attacks invite counterattacks.
- Not listening invites increased irritation.
- Avoidance invites increased frustration.
- Rhetorical questions invite others to resentfully justify themselves.
- Overwhelming the other person invites them to shrivel up and disappear.
- Making demands without making a case for what we need invites the other person to dismiss us as being unreasonable.
- Deception invites more clever deception.
- Acting superior invites competitive one-upmanship.

And the list goes on...

The Stomach Knows

How can we tell if our behavior is making the other person defensive? Our stomach tells us. If we are feeling:

- We want to beat the other person.
- We want someone to pay.
- We want them to admit they are wrong or it is their fault.
- We want to win...

Chances are that our behavior is blocking a successful resolution. We know in our bodies whether we are in a win/lose posture or whether we are in a posture of wanting to understand the other person so we can reach a mutual solution.

Winning and resolving are not synonymous. When we want to be the winner (and want someone else to lose), we are usually behaving in ways that prevent the other person from cooperating with us. We get the responses that we set up. When we accuse the other person of being inflexible, it is likely we ourselves are being inflexible and setting the other person up to dig in and become stubborn.

The reality is that sometimes we don't want to negotiate. We want to beat someone—and the price we will have to pay for beating him is worth it to us. We may be angry with a client and consequently tell her what she can do with her business. We may be willing to pay the price not only of lost business, but also of the 'bad press' we may get with other clients.

When that is the case, we take our sugar and our lumps. We shouldn't kid ourselves. We need to be honest with ourselves about what we are doing so we can realistically assess whether the price we pay for beating the other person is worth it.

Introverts And Extroverts

Often, we are not aware of the impact our behavior has on others. Take for example Extroverts and Introverts. Extroverts think out loud. If they have a problem, they need to talk about it with someone. They think on their feet. Introverts, on the other hand, think internally. If they have a problem, their tendency is to go off and ponder it by themselves, decide on a course of action, and do it. It doesn't occur to them that others have not been part of their thought process, that the validity of their decisions may not be obvious to others. They are surprised when others are not automatically on their bandwagon.

Extroverts and Introverts drive each other bonkers. Introverts do not understand that Extroverts are just thinking out loud, that they're not stating final conclusions or making commitments. As Introverts, they don't open their mouths until they have it all figured out.

Extroverts, on the other hand, become suspicious of Introverts because Introverts want time to go off by themselves and think about it. Extroverts think the Introverts may be stalling and they don't know what they are thinking. The more uneasy the Extroverts get, the more they press to talk about it now, piling on more questions and more data. This, in turn, overwhelms the Introverts, who need more time to withdraw and think. And the dance goes on.

What to do? If you are an Extrovert:

1. Shut up more often.

2. Slow down on all your data and questions.
3. Give them time to think. Remember, you don't always have to finish the negotiation in one session.
4. Check out your assumptions rather than act on the belief they are doing something underhanded.
5. Let them know when you are making commitments and when you are just thinking out loud.

If you are an Introvert:

1. Check out #5 above.
2. Take a break so you have time to think and let them know when you will come back to them, so they don't think you are stalling.
3. When you have thought it through and reached a decision, tell them how you arrived at your conclusion and what you perceive that solution will do for you. *They can't read your mind.* If you don't tell them, you may not like what they read into your intentions.

The Old Parental "Why" Question

Another behavior pattern that produces defensiveness is "Why" questions. Ever have your parents ask you "why" you did something that they didn't approve of and found they weren't asking a real question? They just wanted you to feel guilty? "Why did you get dirty?" or "Why did you stay out so late?" or "Why didn't you call me and tell me you were drunk and not coming home?" (Answer: "Because I'm not that dumb!")

Parents love to ask "Why" questions. But they aren't questions. They're indictments.

When we feel like parental adults, we have a tendency to do the same thing with other adults. "Why would you do that?" or "Why did you turn that way?" or "Why didn't you . . . ?" or "Why don't you just . . . ?" or "I don't understand why you . . . ?"

"Why" questions are usually indirect statements of anger, not authentic questions seeking objective understanding of the facts. If you really want to further understanding between yourself and others, ask what—"What happened?" or "What is your thinking about that suggestion?" or "What do you need?" or "What led you to that decision?"

"What" questions, provided they are real questions and asked without sarcasm, will usually elicit factual responses. "Why" questions, even if they are intended as factual questions, usually make the other person feel like a guilty child.

Avoid Seductive Blaming

Seductive blaming is another cause of defensive behavior. Seductive blaming occurs when someone asks you for information and uses it against you to make the situation your fault. For example, as your employer, I might ask what you are feeling after a staff meeting and then use that data to blame you directly or indirectly. It's as if I've already held the trial in my head and now I'm gathering the data to support my assumptions.

The obvious message here is that if you don't want to constrict the other person's thinking, have the trial before the hanging. Check out your assumptions before acting on them.

Triggering Events

Another behavioral factor which produces defensiveness in negotiations is a triggering event. A triggering event is whatever immediate behavior notifies us that we have a problem or conflict that needs to be addressed. A triggering event may be what someone does or what someone fails to do.

Possible triggering events are:

- Receiving a complaining phone call.
- Receiving a letter from a client informing us that they do not intend to pay a bill.
- The look on someone's face or her tone of voice.
- Having someone bring up a hidden agenda item during a meeting.
- Being put off when you want a meeting.
- Having people be accommodating when we don't believe they really agree with us.

Any behavior might be a triggering event; it is whatever signals us to pay attention. As such, triggering events are gifts. They are usually annoying, but gifts nonetheless. They tell us we need to listen, to focus on what is occurring. They give us information we need.

At the same time, we don't want to lock into the triggering event. We don't want to respond with lower level behavior. Triggering events are symptoms, but not the real issue. They point to the real issues.

To lock into trigger behavior is usually not productive. When we do this, our tendency is to degenerate into a blame game that goes nowhere but down. "I don't like your tone of voice." "Well, I don't like your tone of voice either!" "Well, I don't like your mother." "I never liked your mother either!"

Instead of locking into the triggering behavior, accept it as an annoying gift that is telling us something we need to know. Accept the triggering event as an important source of information. Look through the behavior. Listen to what the other persons are saying about what their problem is and what they need.

Use the triggering behavior to move toward resolution. Don't use it against yourself by locking into it. Focus on the meaning of the behavior, not the behavior itself.

Check out what the other person's tone of voice means or what it is he wants to say with his rhetorical question. Find out why you didn't get invited to the party and address the underlying issue. Describe the triggering behavior to the other person and check out your assumptions. Let the other person know how his behavior is affecting you and what you need.

For example:

- When the other person says she doesn't have time to fulfill your request, find out what "doesn't have time" means before assuming she is just lazy.
- When the other person jumps on you with his anger, find out what is causing his anger and what he needs and wants from you before jumping on him with your anger.
- When an employee doesn't meet the deadline, find out what prevented her before accusing her of having a bad attitude.
- When your spouse says he doesn't want to talk about it, find out what he needs to be able to talk about it. Don't assume he does not want to resolve the conflict.

- When your client calls up and accuses you of doing a shoddy job, find out what happened before you start justifying yourself.
- When someone remains silent, find out what her silence means before accusing her of stalling.
- When you get a letter from a client who is refusing to pay his bill, find out what he's upset about before assuming he is a deadbeat and turning him over to a collection agency.
- When your partner accuses you of being uncooperative, ask her what you are doing that conveys that message before retaliating with counter-accusations.

For more examples of behaviors that cause people to be defensive rather than cooperative, and ways of dealing with them, see Chapters 4, 6, 8, and 10.

A "TO DO" LIST FOR CREATING SAFE ENVIRONMENTS

- Stay in Generative capacities.
- Identify other people's behavior and thinking levels. Assess their behavior and decide what is threatening them and what they need.
- Consider the environmental factors affecting them.
- Ask yourself what is preventing them from doing what you want them to do.
- Consider who their constituency is—and what you can do to help them go home looking good.
- Don't be locked into being a jerk. If you surprise them by being reasonable, you may surprise them into being reasonable themselves.
- Make it as easy as possible for them to cooperate with you.
- Consider whether your requests are unreasonable. Would you be willing to do what you expect them to do?

- Listen to other people's underlying beliefs. Assess whether they are operating from present data or past experiences.
- Confront, if necessary.
- Don't plan your defense while they are talking.
- Check whether your behavior is making them defensive.
- Avoid getting locked into triggering events.
- Ask yourself what you can do to make it easier for them to cooperate with you.
- Don't ask "why" questions. Ask "what" questions.
- Keep the problem out there instead of personalizing it and getting defensive.
- Focus on what you have in common before focusing on your differences. Let them know what you agree with and make additional comments rather than beginning, "You're wrong" or "I don't agree with you."
- Stay focused in the present ("What do you need and what would you like me to do?") rather than arguing over who said what in the past. Be aware that Getting the Facts Straight often means "I want you to admit it has all been your fault."
- Identify and acknowledge what you have contributed to the problem before expecting them to hang themselves.
- Listen to the meaning of other people's behavior. Don't react to their external behavior. Remember: you are dealing with kids running around in adult bodies. Listen to what those kids are telling you they need and respond to that. Make it safe for them to cooperate with you.

CHAPTER 13

PRINCIPLE #2: SHIFT YOUR FOCUS

In every negotiation, we are dealing with four factors.

THE FOUR FACTORS

1. The Substantive Issue (the Problem—what we are talking about).
2. The Relationship (the Conflict—the degree of acceptance or nonacceptance by the other person).
3. The Process (how we are talking or not talking to each other to solve the problem and resolve the relationship).
4. The Criteria (the standards for settlement).

For example:

1. We may be talking about the compensation system in our organization (the substantive issue or problem). (Factor 1)
2. I may feel resentful toward you because I believe you are trying to take advantage of me (that's the conflict or nonacceptance in our relationship). (Factor 2)
3. We may be yelling at each other and not listening and bringing up past events (the process we are using). (Factor 3)
4. I may be citing industry standards for my type of position, and you may be arguing about the tradition

of compensation policies in this organization (the standards for fair settlement). (Factor 4)

1. Sometimes the primary issue is the substantive issue and that's what we need to focus on. (Factor 1)
2. Sometimes the primary issue is our relationship—either because it is more important than the problem, or because we have a conflict and unless we address the conflict, it will make it more difficult or even impossible to solve the problem. (Factor 2)
3. Sometimes the process needs to be negotiated first because the way we try to solve the problem gets us pitted against each other and stuck. (Factor 3)
4. Sometimes we need to agree to fair criteria for settlement before we talk about the substantive issue because you want to get everything you can out of me whether it is fair or not. (Factor 4)

Our tendency in a negotiation is only to talk about the problem, the substantive issue, and ignore:

- The quality of the relationship with the other person.
- The process we are using to negotiate with each other.
- What each of us believes would be fair criteria for settlement.

Effective negotiators realize they must shift their focus among these four factors. At various times in a negotiation, each of these factors may be the primary issue that needs to be addressed. It is important to know when to focus on the problem, when to focus on the relationship, when to focus on the process, and when to focus on the criteria for settlement.

In this chapter, I will explain each of these factors and give you some criteria for deciding when you need to shift your focus. By not appropriately shifting our focus in a negotiation, we get blocked or stuck because we are not talking about the right issue at the right time.

SEPARATE PROBLEMS FROM CONFLICTS

In every negotiation we are dealing with substantive issues and relationship issues. Substantive issues are the problems. They are the external conditions, behaviors, events, or objects that we want or we want to change. They may be the procedures being used, the secretary who is not producing, the cash flow, the competition moving in across the street, the terms of the union contract, the non-payment of an overdue account, or the lack of service for the computer we've installed.

While trying to negotiate solutions to problems, people often develop mistrust and misunderstanding. Their negotiating process gets bogged down or stopped because conflicts arise. Conflicts are related to the quality of the relationship between the negotiating persons. Conflicts have to do with what people believe and feel about each other. Conflict is synonymous with nonacceptance. People are in conflict when they do not accept each other's feelings or needs—or when they do not accept each other's beliefs or perceptions.

In every negotiation, substantive issues and relationship issues have a relative importance. Sometimes the problem is most important to us, and the people involved are of lesser importance. This may be true in negotiating a union contract or when purchasing a piece of equipment. We may not know the other people or care about them, or ever plan to see them again.

At other times, the person may be more important to us than the problem. We may have a problem with our production manager's behavior, but we do not want to lose him. We may be negotiating with a client to pay her overdue account. If this particular client represents 20 percent of our gross business, our ongoing relationship may be much more important that getting everything we want from the immediate situation.

It is helpful to clarify for ourselves the relative weight or importance of the problem we are addressing versus our relationship with the other person. Determining the relative importance of the problem gives us a measure of how far we want to push to get our results. It also gives us information about the focus we want to assume in our negotiation. Whenever the other person is important to us, we are doing more than simply negotiating a problem. We are also negotiating a relationship.

Our negotiating will sometimes be focused primarily on solving problems. Other times we will be focused on resolving conflicts. *During a successful negotiation process, we will usually be focusing on solving a problem and on resolving a relationship.* Conflicts often arise in the course of negotiating solutions to problems. When this happens, we need to shift the focus of the negotiation from problem-solving to resolving relationship issues.

Notice how the focus shifts back and forth in the following dialogue between two partners in an engineering firm.

Problem Focus:

Tom: Do you have a minute to talk?

Drew: Sure.

Tom: I've been reading over the results from our marketing survey. We've gotten consistent comments from your clients that they were frustrated because their projects were not completed on schedule. I'm concerned about the long-term effects of these comments on our reputation and on future referrals.

Drew: There weren't that many comments. One or two, maybe.

Tom: Well, actually there were five comments—and I received a phone call from Lewis Brothers. That represents 75 percent of the clients you've worked with over the past six months. I think that adds up to a problem.

Drew: Some of them were really not that late.

Tom: I don't know how late any of them were. That would be easy enough to document, but that's not the issue. I'm aware of two things right now. One is that clients thought it was too late, and they make up our referral base.

Relationship Focus:

Tom: The second issue I'm aware of is that it doesn't feel like we're on the same side of the table. My intention in talking with you is not to accuse or blame you. I simply want to solve what I see as a problem. I'm not asking you to justify what you've done. I want to work together to see what we can do to prevent this problem from occurring in the future.

Problem Focus:

Drew: Well, I guess I did get behind in the past few months. I don't know why.
Tom: Were there problems with the projects? Did you have too much to do?
Drew: Not really. Nothing unusual.
Tom: Something must be going on.
Drew: I don't know what it is. Beats me.

Relationship Focus:

Tom: I'm feeling frustrated. I don't think we are getting any place. We have a problem, and it has to do with your level of output. Right now it seems to me that you're playing dumb, hoping I'll get tired and go away. I need to know what's going on. I'd like to hear some specific answers.
Drew: I haven't felt much like working since last summer.
Tom: What's that about?
Drew: I don't feel like putting a lot of work into the partnership when your family is taking all the profits.
Tom: Are you angry because I hired my son last summer?
Drew: I'm angry that you didn't ask me first.
Tom: That was my mistake. I'm sorry about that. We needed the help and you were out of town. Is that the real reason why your productivity has been down?

Problem focus:

Drew: That's really only a small part of it. I've had a lot of pressure at home. My son has been having problems, and Alice has been on my back. I've had trouble concentrating on my work. I guess I've been procrastinating a lot.

Tom: I'm sorry to hear that. Is there anything I can do?

Drew: Not really. I knew I wasn't getting stuff done, but I didn't think anyone else had noticed. I need to talk to Alice and get some things resolved—and I need to leave home at home. Now that we've talked about it, I guess I'm more conscious of what's been happening. I'll take care of it.

Tom: Thanks. Let's talk again in a couple of weeks and see where we are then. In the meantime, let me know if you need anything.

Drew: Thanks, I will.

Our tendency in a negotiation is to stay focused on the problem and avoid the conflict. This is usually a mistake. It feels more threatening to confront our relationship with another person than to talk about the problem. However, if we don't confront the relationship issue, that conflict will often prevent us from solving the problem or make it much more difficult to do so. If we are angry with the other person and believe he is trying to cheat us, we may never reach a settlement.

Addressing conflicts that exist is essential to resolving the immediate situation, and it also lays groundwork for the future. In the example above, Tom kept the negotiations moving by shifting his focus between the problem (Drew's output), their relationship (Drew's anger about Tom hiring his son), and the process (Drew avoiding and playing dumb). If Tom had not been aware of the various factors (the problem, the relationship, and the process), if he had focused only on what was immediately going on, they would not have reached resolution. It was Tom's awareness and his willingness to shift the focus that made the negotiation successful.

Not resolving relationship issues often results in new problems arising in the future or in prior agreements not being kept. If we believe another person has taken advantage of us in the past, we're going to be looking for ways to even the score. Many people have experienced the revengeful behavior of a former business partner, employee, or spouse who feels they were cheated or used or betrayed. When that happens, we usually have a repeating pattern of problems with that person.

Another reason for addressing conflicts as they arise is that sometimes the problem is simply a camouflage—the symptom of a relationship conflict. I may not be getting your work done because we have a breakdown in our relationship. I may have heard that you made derogatory comments about me to one of my clients. If this is the case, solving the immediate problem won't accomplish much. Rather, we need to address the conflict. When we do, the problem will probably go away.

For example:

Judy and Bob started a business together seven years ago. Judy had worked very had to make the business go while at the same time giving birth to three children and caring for them. Without her contribution and her organizational skills, the business would not have gotten off the ground. But Bob is not one to give recognition and he tends to talk in public as if the business were all his doing.

While Judy is no longer involved in the business full-time or in a formal way, she is interested in product development. She frequently shows up at product development meetings to offer her opinions.

The research and development director told Judy that her participation was valuable but sometimes disruptive because she was not present at all the meetings. He asked that she either not come at all, or (he preferred this) that she formally become a member of the Research and Development Committee and attend all its meetings.

Judy was angry and shot back at the research and development director that it was her company and she'd do what she wanted. She went on to express her resentment about not being valued appropriately ("After all I've done!"), and with that, she walked out and slammed the door.

The research and development director was surprised at the strength of her reaction. What he didn't know was the history of her relationship with Bob. What he didn't know was that 10 percent of her response had to do with him, and 90 percent had to do with her unresolved conflicts with Bob.

The primary issue here was not Judy's participation on the committee. The primary issue was her unresolved relationship with Bob. Until that was resolved, a whole series of problems cropped up concerning her involvement in different parts of the company's operation.

The research and development director reported to Bob what had happened. Bob went home, asked what the problem was—and found out. It took them a week and several ventings and discussions, but they resolved the conflict. Judy's involvement in the research and development meetings became a non-issue. She really didn't want to be involved in the business any longer. She simply wanted to be recognized for her past contribution.

In this example, the people involved were important to each other. However, even if the other person is not particularly important to us, it makes sense to resolve conflicts as they arise. By resolving our conflicts, we will resolve our present problems more easily. We will remove the blocks that often keep us from solving our problems. If the conflict involves a client, we will keep a potential referral source instead of having bad press following us around—and we just never know when we might need that referral source in the future.

Knowing When To Shift

How do we know when we have a conflict that needs to be addressed? We know that we have simply a problem when we can both sit down together, define the problem, analyze the causes, brainstorm potential solutions, and decide on possible strategies for responding to the problem. We know we have simply a problem when it feels as if we are working together and the problem stays out there.

We know we probably have a conflict when:

- We feel we are pushing against each other instead of cooperating.
- We start getting defensive or angry.
- We can't solve the problem because we can't work together.
- We have a repeating pattern of problems.
- The same problem keeps emerging.

Basically, we know in our guts when we have a conflict—it's when those old win/lose feelings start bubbling up inside us. It's when we want to blame the other person and do not want to admit that anything is our fault.

Compromise Versus Acceptance

Solving problems is not the same as resolving conflicts. *What will solve a problem will not necessarily resolve a conflict.* Each requires different resources. Problems are external to us and quantitative in nature. They can usually be measured in dollars, time, materials, space, or behavior. The solving of problems usually takes one or more of these quantitative resources. We need more money or more time or more machinery or more space or different behaviors or more staff.

The reality of our physical world is that we are often faced with limited material resources. We have only so much money and a limited number of staff. That means we must compromise in order to solve the problem.

But compromise never works for resolving a conflict. Conflicts are caused by a lack of understanding and acceptance. Conflicts are resolved when both persons understand and accept each other in the moment. The resource which resolves conflicts is *acceptance.* Acceptance is an unlimited resource. We choose whether or not to understand and accept who the other person is. *Because of this choice, every conflict is resolvable—if we want to resolve it.*

The conflict between Judy and Bob was resolved when both of them sat down and expressed what they were feeling and needing—and had their feelings and needs not only understood but accepted by the other person.

I encounter this type of situation daily in organizations with which I work. As an organizational development consultant, I am frequently called on to solve organizational "problems." Very often, the real issue is an unresolved relationship conflict.

For example:

Jim was the department head of plant maintenance. Carl was the plant supervisor of maintenance in one of the facilities and reported to Jim. I was asked to help solve Carl's performance problems, which were ascribed to incompetence.

After the initial interview, it was clear that work was not being completed up to standards, but it was not clear that the primary cause was Carl's incompetence. Several factors contributed to the lack of results—outdated and obsolete equipment, unclear definition of roles and job responsibilities, unstated expectations by Jim, and a long history of distrust and avoidance by both men in addressing their relationship.

Both men were resentful, both felt unfairly criticized, both believed the other person was out to get him, and neither of them accepted any responsibility for the problem. Clearly, until the relationship issue was addressed and resolved, the problems could not be solved. In this instance, Carl was not willing to talk about their relationship.

Sometimes this is the reality. Sometimes we find ourselves in situations where the other person is not willing to address the conflict. Even if the other person is not ready or willing to accept us, we can still get resolution. It is easier if they cooperate, but it is not necessary.

Our resolution does not depend upon others. It depends upon our choices.

Acceptance of the fact that they do not want to resolve relationship issues is in itself a resolution. Once we accept the fact that the other person is neither willing nor able to understand and accept us, we are free to move on and do whatever it is we need to do to take care of ourselves. Resolution happens when we stop expecting something that isn't going to happen.

Again, it is important to know when we are dealing with simply a problem or when we also have a conflict. Compromise can help solve some problems, but it never resolves a conflict. Compromise and acceptance are based on different assumptions. Compromise is based on the belief that:

- We have limited resources (true with problems).

- There is not enough of anything for everyone to have everything they want (sometimes true when we are talking about physical resources).
- Someone has to give up part of what they want.

We see why compromise does not work for resolving relationship issues. If the cause of a conflict is a lack of understanding and acceptance of who we are, to compromise means we are willing to be less than who we are. We are willing to accept less value or worth for ourselves. That never works.

We are either accepted or we are not. Partial acceptance means the conflict is not resolved. *Compromise can work for solving problems. Only acceptance resolves conflicts.*

But acceptance should not be confused with resignation. Acceptance means we believe they are doing what they are capable of doing, given who they are. But acceptance does not mean that we allow ourselves to be victimized by them. It does mean we accept the present reality. But to accept the present reality does not mean we decide to stay in it.

Resignation, on the other hand, is not acceptance. It is giving up. In resignation, we haven't accepted the reality of the situation. We have given up trying to get what we need. We resent the other person and blame them for preventing us from getting what we need. We give them unreal power over us. We shift the responsibility for ourselves onto them.

Resignation is what we do on the lower levels. We give up (Stage 1); we scheme to get back at them in the future (Stage 2); we try to make the situation go away by being pleasing and accommodating (Stage 3); or we flip them off (Stage 4). In resignation, the conflict is still alive and well—it has just gone underground.

When I hear someone say, "We have agreed to disagree," I hear two possible messages. On one hand it may be true—they mutually respect and accept each other's differing perspectives. On the other hand, what I hear (usually from the sarcasm in the person's voice) is that neither accepts the other's differing perspectives, and both feel stuck. They don't know how to resolve it. They have an unresolved conflict and have become resigned.

Acceptance is different from agreement. Agreement implies that we not only understand and accept why other people are doing what they are doing, we also support them in doing it, even at our own cost. Acceptance does not mean we allow ourselves to be victimized by them. It only means that we accept the reality of who they are. We may also have to draw boundaries with them.

For example:

I can understand and accept that an employee is under a lot of stress from home because her husband is an invalid and they are under financial strain, but this doesn't mean that I continue to allow her to perform her job poorly. I can understand and accept the reasons for her low productivity, but acceptance does not mean that I also agree to pay the price for her low productivity.

In the same way, I understand my kid's need to impress his girl friend. That doesn't mean I'm willing to buy him a sports car. Acceptance and agreement are two different realities.

Acceptance is what we do on level five as generators. We accept what is and we either work with that reality or we move on to take care of ourselves in other ways. We know when we have reached a point of acceptance when we feel resolved and peaceful inside rather than resentful.

Acceptance requires that we use our capacity for empathy—to get inside the other person and to know what it is like to be them, to know what they need. *Again, only acceptance resolves conflicts and acceptance is our choice.*

An example that illustrates real resolution occurred with one of my sons. Jay, who was seventeen at the time, had not been doing his house chores, which were supposed to be completed by noon on Saturdays. I felt frustrated, resentful, and used and assumed that Jay was just avoiding his responsibilities.

When we sat down to talk, we first went through several minutes (more like forty-five) accusing and judging each other. "You're not being responsible." "You're not listening to me." "You're not being fair."

Finally, we did begin listening to each others' needs. I finally understood the amount of pressure Jay was feeling going to school and working twenty-five hours a week and realized that Saturday morning was his only day to sleep late. It seemed reasonable that he didn't want to spend Saturday morning working around the house before going to work at his job at noon.

He, in turn, accepted my need to have the jobs done every week. At that point, we both felt listened to, respected, understood, and accepted. The solution to the problem came easily—he agreed to do them on Sunday afternoons. It wasn't that he was unwilling to do the chores, as I had assumed. It was a matter of timing.

Key Points To Remember In Separating Problems From Conflicts

1. It is important to separate problems from conflicts—to know what we need to focus on and when we need to shift our focus.
2. Our tendency is to stay focused on solving problems and to avoid relationship conflicts. But we pay a price and the price is usually much higher that what it would cost us to resolve a conflict now.
3. As long as we have an unresolved conflict with someone, he OWNS a part of us. As long as we are angry with someone, the part of us that is angry is not available to us—it is focused on the other person. That person uses up our time and energy—time and energy that could be spent on meeting our own needs.
4. We need to distinguish between compromising and accepting. Compromise can work for solving problems. Only acceptance resolves conflicts.
5. We should not confuse acceptance with resignation or agreement.
6. Conflicts can only be resolved by Generator behavior. Only Generators have the ability to accurately see both sides, to see through the behavior of others, and to understand and accept the limitations of a given situation. Only Generators trust themselves enough to accept the limitations in others and to move on and take care of themselves responsibly.

7. As Generators, we deal with both problems and relationships in all negotiations. As Generators, we are able to shift our focus back and forth and advance the negotiation.

FOCUS ON PROCESS

Sometimes in a negotiation we need to address the Process or Criteria before addressing either the Problem or the Relationship. This is particularly true when we are negotiating with Scorekeepers, but it may be true when we are dealing with anyone on the lower four levels of thinking.

The reason we need to address the Process and Criteria up-front with Scorekeepers is because of their tendency to be deceptive. Negotiating with a Scorekeeper is like playing cards with someone who doesn't tell you what all the rules are up-front and keeps changing the rules to suit himself along the way.

As pointed out in earlier chapters, we see this type of deception or maneuvering often in our negotiations. We see it in:

- The person who claims she would like to cooperate, but her partner or the committee or the Board, who are not present, would never agree to it.
- The person who keeps putting you off and stalling.
- The person who is locked into a position and refuses to budge.
- The person who disowns responsibility for whatever is nonproductive or dysfunctional.
- The person who refuses to talk.
- The person who keeps attacking and blaming.
- The person who insists there is one right answer—hers.
- The person who agrees with you to your face and then goes off and does something else.

Often in our negotiations, the process we are using blocks us from reaching a mutually satisfying agreement. When this is the case, the rule of thumb is that we need to negotiate the process before talking about the relationship or the specific content or problem.

Some examples:

If a person tends to make a scene and walk away, set up your discussion so he can't do this easily. Meet him in a restaurant or have your discussion in the car while you are driving.

When a person becomes locked in a position, don't get locked into an opposing position ("You *will* have it done by noon on Saturday!"). Discover what underlying needs prevent her from doing what you want. Ask what her position means to her so you can understand why she is adopting her stance.

When a person refuses to talk, point out that as long as he is silent, neither of you will get what you want.

When a person is attacking and blaming, don't follow suit, change the process by asking him to tell you more about what he is dissatisfied with and what it is he would like to have from you.

When a person wants to change the terms of a contract at the last minute, point out her behavior and put off the closing time. Tell her you are not willing to be held up or pressured into an unsatisfactory agreement at the last minute. Have her tell you whether she is willing to stick to her agreement before talking about the terms again.

When a person insists there is only one right answer, point out that by doing this she eliminates the possibility of choosing from multiple solutions. She is limiting her options. Ask her if she would be willing to explore the possibility that there are several valid solutions to the problem.

If you are negotiating with someone who avoids the issue by never giving you his full attention, suggest that you meet someplace else where there won't be any distractions or interruptions.

If you find yourself in an argument where both you and the other person are justifying your own behavior and blaming each other, stop and focus on the process by saying: "Sounds as if we are each defending ourselves and wanting to make each other wrong. I don't think we are going to reach agreement this way." Then proceed by admitting what you are contributing to the problem. Be accountable for your own behavior. This usually makes it safe for the other person to do the same.

When you find yourself in a meeting in which people are personalizing the issues and defending themselves, point out what you see going on and suggest that it might be more productive to step back and focus on the problem as a common issue that needs to be solved. "I wonder what each of us would need to be able to work together and solve our common problem."

If you and the other person find that it is impossible to talk without getting stuck or blocked, suggest using a third-party facilitator.

The principle is: when what you are doing in a negotiation is not working, stop. Step back. Point out the behaviors that are preventing you from reaching resolution and suggest an alternative process.

WHEN TO FOCUS ON THE CRITERIA

The same principle holds true for the criteria or standards we believe determine a fair settlement. When it becomes clear in a negotiation that you and the other party are using different criteria or operating from different values, focus on reaching mutual agreement about fair criteria or common values before trying to negotiate the problem or relationship.

Some examples:

If you have a car accident and need to negotiate the insurance settlement with an adjuster, do your homework first by getting estimates on the damage and the value of your car. Alternative sources for determining the value of your car include automobile dealers, independent appraisals, newspaper advertisements, and lending institutions. Once you have your data, don't talk about the actual value of your car (the problem), negotiate what the term "full coverage" means in your policy and which of your sources will be a mutually agreeable standard for determining the value of your car. Lock the adjuster into fair criteria first.

If you are negotiating for a piece of real estate, be aware that since real estate values have declined in many areas over the past few years, sellers tend to value their property according to 1979 property values. Again, do your homework, and be clear with the seller that you are negotiating based on current values, not 1979 values.

If you want to develop a more productive and cooperative work team, get them to agree to common values about the kind of work environment they would like to have and their criteria for success. "Given our past history and the future demands facing us, what do we believe will determine whether or not we achieve our goals?" Then translate those goals into behavioral indexes—"If we are living by these values, what will we be doing individually and as a team? What behaviors will manifest these values?"

If you want to assign household chores, get some agreement about the standard of living everyone wants, then decide what tasks are required to achieve this standard, then decide the criteria for dividing up these tasks (fair, equal, require same amount of time, will take into account individual needs and preferences). Then and only then negotiate who will do what.

These same principles apply whether you are talking about international disarmament, child custody, product quality, contractual terms, or employee performance.

As we see from these examples, it is necessary to get agreement about fair standards or common values up front. And usually we have a variety of possible sources for these criteria, such as:

- Personal experience or needs
- Experts or recognized authorities
- Industry requirements
- Laws
- Market values
- Wholesale or rental indexes
- Tradition

KEY POINTS TO REMEMBER

When you wonder what to focus on in a negotiation, keep in mind your four major topics or factors:

1. The Problem
2. The Relationship
3. The Process
4. The Criteria

If you and the other party cannot sit down and cooperatively solve the problem together, you know you need to focus on one of the other three factors.

As a General Rule:

1. Negotiate the process—how you are going to talk to each other—first.
2. Make sure you are in agreement about the criteria to be used for a fair settlement.
3. Listen to your stomach. If you feel defensive, if you feel like fighting, you both probably need to develop some mutual understanding and acceptance before trying to tackle the problem.
4. Only after you have negotiated the first three factors are you ready to address the content or problem. If you have done a good job resolving the process, criteria, and relationship, solving the problem is usually a piece of cake. Try it. You may like the way it tastes.

CHAPTER 14

PRINCIPLE #3: UNDERSTAND OTHERS, DON'T BEAT THEM

DISTINGUISH BETWEEN PROBLEMS AND SOLUTIONS

The failure to distinguish between *problems* and *solutions* is a major cause for unsuccessful negotiations. The principle is: focus on defining the problem and not on defending solutions.

The distinction between problems, needs, values, concerns, and interests, on the one hand, and solutions, answers, or satisfactory behavior, on the other hand, may seem obvious to you theoretically. But these two categories often get confused in the heat of debate.

The One Hand:	*The Other Hand:*
Problems & Needs	**Solutions**
To not have personal liability for an office copy machine.	To not sign a personal note for the purchase of a copy machine.
Loss of market share.	Reorganization of the marketing department.
Water in your basement.	Fix the window wells or re-landscape the yard.

Management team in conflict and not working cooperatively.	Do some team building, resolve the conflicts, transfer key people.
To know our teenagers are safe.	Establish consequences for drinking and driving.
To have satisfied customers.	Train our receptionists in customer satisfaction skills.
To feel valued and respected.	To be asked instead of told to do a task.

We decide on answers and solutions, we adopt stands, because we have underlying needs we wish to meet. Behind every solution is a need.

- We confront our boss for a raise (the solution) because we need to feel valued—we need to feel we are being paid what we are worth.
- We file suit to collect a delinquent account (solution) because we don't want to feel we've been a patsy, and we need the money.
- We decide to take on a partner (solution) because we need someone to collaborate with, to stimulate our creativity.

The distinction between problems and solutions is important. It is important for two reasons:

1. By ignoring underlying problems or needs, we usually fail to come up with our best options.
2. By focusing on solutions rather than problems, we usually TAKE A STAND to promote or defend our solution. We assume we have the right answer or best solution because we thought of it.

Once we have taken a stand, we tend to identify our personal worth, our self-esteem, with that stand. And once we have aligned our self-worth with our stand, then we often end up negotiating about our self-worth rather than the underlying problem. Our negotiation ends up being a contest to prove who's right or who's stronger.

Define The Problem Before Jumping To Solutions

By prematurely focusing on solutions, we often fail to adequately identify what we need. We fail to develop a complete and accurate understanding of the problem.

- We are likely to come up with solutions that will not fully solve the problem—the wrong solutions.
- We tend to limit our creativity and options. We fail to see all the possible ways in which our needs might get met.

It is important that we clearly analyze our situation before jumping to solutions.

For example:

The owners of a communications firm were having repeated cash flow problems. Clients were slow to pay their bills (ninety days) but the firm's equipment suppliers wanted payment within thirty days. The only solution the owners perceived was to generate more business. They went out and hunted up additional clients, hired another person, and started working evenings and weekends.

But the problem didn't go away. In fact, it became more complicated. The firm's volume had increased but so had their overhead. In addition, clients were frustrated because the firm was unable to keep up with the volume of work. The owners felt overwhelmed, which made them less productive, and their suppliers were still demanding payment. There seemed to be no solution.

The owners asked for help. They met with their accountant and a management consultant. They began to see that the source of the problem was not a lack of volume—it was timing. They needed to establish a policy of payment with their clients, and they needed to negotiate a different payment policy with their suppliers.

So they did. They established a policy of receiving one-third payment at the time a contract was signed and one-third when the project was completed. The balance was due thirty days from the project completion date. The owners negotiated with their supplier to pay him thirty days after a project was completed rather than thirty days after the equipment was delivered. Because they took the time to analyze the source of the problem, the problem was solved.

Solutions are only as good as our prior problem analysis. Solutions are only good if they solve the real problem.

UNDERSTAND THE NEEDS ON BOTH SIDES

Focusing on the problem, not the solution, is crucial in developing solutions that work and in expanding our options. Just because we thought of a solution does not mean it is the only solution. We can almost always come up with more ideas and better solutions by collaborating with others.

Our primary task in a negotiation is not to come up with the right answer. Our task is to get the real problem identified and the real underlying needs understood and accepted. Solutions are easy. *Solutions naturally come into focus once we have identified the real needs.*

For example:

My son Aaron and I argued over whether he would buy a car. I said "No" because he didn't have enough money saved. He was determined to buy a car and he wanted me to give him the money.

When we finally sat down to talk reasonably, I pointed out my values and needs. I wanted him to learn to live within his means and to be responsible, and I wanted him to pay for the car. He, in turn, explained that he had a job offer which would enable him to pay off the car in six months, but he needed the car to get the job. He also laid out the data he had gathered, namely, detailed information on the cost of insurance and a car loan from his credit union (he already had the loan approved). By anticipating my needs (he knows me pretty well), he had come up with a solution that would meet both our needs. I couldn't argue with his solution. He had expanded our options.

As my experience with Aaron points out, it is important to focus on understanding the needs of both parties. By leading off with solutions, we set up our negotiation to be a win/lose bargaining process. We focus only on what we want and fail to understand what the other person needs.

Entering a negotiation with a firm stand or position invites the other person to be defensive. He immediately feels the need to counter our stand so he won't lose. The focus of the negotiation becomes winning or being right rather than understanding and cooperatively searching for creative solutions. Energy spent on winning is energy lost.

The primary task in every negotiation is to understand the other person—not to beat him. We need to look behind his behavior and find out why he is doing what he is doing. We need to find out why he has adopted his stand and what he needs to have in order to give us what we want.

We need to realize that whatever people do, they do for some good reason. We do not do things that do not make sense to us. *All behavior is purposeful.* Every behavior by every human being is perceived by that person as a means to satisfy some need.

In the most extreme case, a person who attempts suicide sees that act as the most loving, life-giving, nurturing thing he can do, or he would do something else. If he could perceive a better option, he'd take it.

The same is true for all of our less extreme behaviors. We all have reasons for what we do. Our job in a negotiation is to get inside the other person and understand his reasons.

For example:

If I don't want to sign a personal note for my copy machine, I need to understand your need for a secure loan and come up with other collateral from the corporation or redefine the criteria for "a secure loan."

If I want you to work on a project for me and set aside the project you are currently working on, I may need to add additional staff or change the expectations related to the completion of the first project.

If I want you to stop sabotaging my proposals in the executive committee, I may need to be willing to listen to your anger toward me and resolve our relationship conflict.

If I want you to stop avoiding me and to talk to me, I must find out what is making you avoid me now.

If you are a bank officer and I am trying to get a line of credit and you don't understand how I arrived at my figures, I may need to take you to my office, have us both sit down at the computer, and run you through step-by-step how I arrived at them. By taking you through my process, you may then understand.

IDENTIFY THE MULTIPLE INTERESTS

The same principles apply to group negotiations. We need to identify whether the other side has multiple interests. We need to understand their relationships and internal politics. We need to look at the whole picture before we analyze the other group's behavior and before we decide which strategies to use in interacting with them.

For example:

I was involved in a negotiation between an advertising agency and the promoters of a major conference. The chairman of the conference was extremely abusive in her comments, was dissatisfied with everything the agency submitted, and was bringing the project to a standstill.

In talking to several key people on both sides, I found that the chairman had previously quarreled with a member of the ad agency. It appeared that she was evening the score. I also learned that the rest of the conference committee was quite satisfied with the agency's work.

The solutions? We sat down and got the conflict between the two principals resolved. Then the conference continued on schedule.

The needs of the person representing a group may not be the same as the needs of some of the other group members. The group's representative may push for a hard line because of old conflicts or because she wants to prove herself and increase her status in her organization. Other members may want a productive long-term relationship rather than a one-time "big kill."

Find Out Who Has The Power

As part of understanding the other side, we need to find out who has the power to make decisions. The project director may lead you to believe that he has the final authority when in fact his president retains that prerogative. You think you have an agreement and go ahead with the project, but when it comes time for payment, the president demands an adjustment in the bill because he didn't like the final product. He assumes you were working speculatively. You assumed you had a firm contract.

The reverse of this is also true. The middle manager may try to get you to agree to concessions because he must present a specific proposal to his boss. He attempts to lock you into contract terms without making a commitment himself, despite the fact that he has the authority to sign the contract. His strategy keeps you on the defensive.

Find out who has the authority to make decisions before committing yourself. What the other persons need and how they interrelate among themselves is our problem. We sabotage ourselves when we do not understand their needs and strategy. If we do not understand them, we do not know how to intervene appropriately with them.

Mutual Understanding Does Not Equal Being Weak

Working for mutual understanding does not mean being wishy-washy or empty-headed. We need to be clear about what we need and want before going into a negotiation. We need to do our homework so we understand who it is we have to deal with and what they are likely to do.

We need to make sure we are understood by being firm, clear, and specific about our needs. We need to make a case for our needs—to make the other side feel our needs and assess them as valid. We cannot expect them to read our minds. Contrary to popular belief, nice guys who wait for others to notice what they need do not finish first.

At the same time that we are firm and clear about what we need, we want to be flexible about how our needs might get met. We want to go in with an open mind—to see the whole picture and to be open to all the possible ways we might get what we need.

As pointed out in the previous chapter, sometimes we confuse understanding and accepting with agreement. The two are not synonymous. We can understand the pressures the other person is feeling. If we try to understand her behavior, perceptions, and needs, we will better understand her position without being a patsy or a victim. To understand does not mean to give in. It simply means accepting the real issues about which we need to negotiate.

To state this as a paradox: *All negotiation is about needs, not solutions. At the same time, our needs are not negotiable.* What we need, we need. Our task is to understand our mutual and differing needs and then search for creative options to satisfy them. We don't identify the needs so we can then argue about whether they are valid.

As a parent, I am readily guilty of finding out from one of my kids what he needs and then discounting the validity of his needs.

Me: I need to understand why you have decided not to start college this year.

Son: Because I'm burned out on school. It's boring. I need a break. Besides, I don't know what I want to do yet.

Me: I don't think those are valid reasons. You don't need to know what you want to do yet. You've got plenty of time to decide that. You just need to get a good general education. You're not going to get anywhere in the world without an education.

And then I wonder why he doesn't want to talk to me.

Mutual Solutions Do Not Equal Mutual Needs

Searching for mutual solutions does not mean getting everyone to have the same needs. The objectives in the negotiating process are to understand the similar and different needs that exist and then to find satisfactory ways to respond to those needs. Often the fact that we have differing needs is the basis for a successful negotiation.

For example:

Ann and Dolores had run a state-of-the-art secretarial service for a number of years. They were both doing everything: processing the work they contracted to do, managing their own business, and selling their services. Both felt spread too thinly and neither was enjoying the business.

When they began talking about it, Ann stated that she really did not enjoy the management tasks or the selling. Dolores, who was much more outgoing, enjoyed the selling and contracting much more than sitting at the office keyboard. The obvious solution, once they understood this, was to divide the tasks. Ann would stay in the office and churn out the work, while Dolores would spend most of her time managing and marketing the business. Both women were more satisfied and productive.

OPTIONS FOR CREATING OPTIONS

Once we have faced the real issues, created a safe environment, resolved the relationship conflicts, and focused on understanding each other's needs, searching for mutual solutions is the easy part of the negotiating process. In the search for mutual solutions, we want to be on the same side of the table. We want to work together Generatively to create all the possible solutions. We do not want to get stuck in looking for the one right answer or in either/or extremes. We always have multiple options, each with different benefits and cost.

We can create many options. We have several options for creating options.

1. We can use the brainstorming technique of listing all the possible solutions without evaluating or judging them. The objective is to see how long a list we can make. Only after we have listed all our ideas do we go back and evaluate their consequences.

2. We can do some research and find out what others have done. We can be sure we are not the only ones to have faced this problem. Who do we know who has experienced this kind of situation?
3. We can seek out expert advice. Who deals with our type of problem—accountants, attorneys, designers, engineers, psychologists, doctors, management consultants? Would it be worth the fee they charge to get their expert advice? Their broader experience often allows them to see what we cannot see by ourselves.

Once we have generated our options, we want to weigh the relative payoffs of each until we come up with the combination that will give both of us the best results. We want everyone to go home satisfied. Giving up some of what we want in the short term may be to our long-term advantage.

While we may have several needs, only one or two may be essential. For a hospital administrator, getting the medical staff committee to agree to a more reasonable policy for granting staff privileges may be essential to the long-term survival of the organization. If this is the case, the administrator will want to consider what concessions can be given to the committee in return, so they don't feel they are losing everything. The administrator doesn't want the committee to go away feeling frightened about their financial security and future status. It will be important for them to leave with their pride intact.

Don't go for the jugular vein when a finger prick will better serve your interests.

By Way of Summary

Negotiating from a posture of understanding rather than winning invites reciprocal understanding. It removes the primary block to cooperation—ourselves. It enables us to gather the data we need to accurately assess our real situation and it positions us to generate more creative and satisfying options for meeting our needs.

Key points to remember about understanding yourself and others:

1. Distinguish between the problems or needs and the solutions or behavioral responses you want from others.
2. Focus on the needs or problems, not the solutions.
3. Clearly define the problem. Don't jump to a solution.
4. Don't get locked into a stand that prevents you from generating the creative options that might meet everyone's needs.
5. People do what they do for good reasons. To change behavior means you must change the consequences for behavior. If you want them to cooperate, you need to make it worth their while to do so.
6. Identify the other side's multiple interests. Identify the people who have the power to make decisions.
7. You won't lose anything by understanding what other people need. You will lose a great deal if you don't understand their needs and defend your own solutions instead.
8. Understand and accept the reality of other people's needs. Do not uncover their needs and then discount their needs as invalid.
9. The primary task in a negotiation is to understand the other person, not beat him.

CHAPTER 15

PRINCIPLE #4: ATTEND TO THE OBVIOUS

In all negotiating, attending to the obvious is the single most important strategy to use. Negotiating is the art of identifying and removing the blocks that arise as we go about getting what we need. Blocks are always going to arise—in the form of limited resources, our own fears, or the fears of others.

As these blocks arise, we have various options for responding. We can push against them, we can try to sneak our way around them, or we can hope they will go away. These are all possible options, but they are not our best options.

Our best option is to dissolve or melt the block. To do this we must first recognize it. If we can recognize the block when it first rears its ugly head, we don't waste time and we don't unintentionally contribute to making the block stronger and more rigid.

For example:

If the other person is making excuses, we want to recognize this and understand why, rather than push against him so he becomes more defensive and has to make more excuses.

If the other person is making extreme demands, we want to step back and understand what is motivating her behavior before we cave in and make concessions that will encourage her to make more extreme demands.

If the other persons are silent or say they don't have time to talk, ask them what their silence or "not enough time" means.

If you think the other person will get defensive and not listen, tell him what your fears are and get their agreement to try to listen.

If you're not sure about your assumptions and are afraid of being wrong, check them out.

If you don't have agreement about the underlying values or terms for a fair settlement, focus on those terms first.

Once we recognize the block, we have the option of looking through it to the underlying causes. Instead of negotiating from a defensive posture, we can set about addressing the underlying needs that are calling to be met. When we address the underlying needs, the block dissolves.

Our block may be an *internal block*. We may be procrastinating about confronting an employee because we are afraid she will complain to other employees and cause ill feelings. Identifying our underlying fear tells us what we need—we need to know the employee will not create ill feelings among other co-workers.

Knowing what we need lets us choose options for taking care of the need. We can check out the validity of our fear, or we can get an up-front agreement with the employee not to talk to others about our problem.

The block may be *external*, arising out of the other person's needs. She may be refusing to negotiate because I embarrassed her by confronting her in front of others. I may need to acknowledge my insensitivity and apologize and suggest we meet privately in her office.

Attending to the obvious means paying attention to what is foreground: what is immediately, obviously going on before and within us. It means paying attention to what is going on in the moment.

Paying attention to:

- What we are feeling and saying to ourselves.
- What the other person is saying and doing.
- The tone of voice and facial expressions.
- The possible incongruity between what a person is saying and his behavior or tone of voice.
- The impact of environmental factors.
- To the moment when the other person's level of thinking begins to shift and she becomes more defensive.

- Whether we are on the same side of the table resolving a problem.
- Whether we also have a relationship conflict to resolve.
- Whether we need the other person to make more specific, complete statements.
- What ongoing process we are using and the direction in which we are heading.
- Whether we have agreement about our criteria for settlement.
- Whether we have a win/lose feeling in our gut or whether we want to understand the other person.
- Whether we are moving toward or away from resolution.

How To Negotiate With A Broad View

Attending to the obvious requires multiple perspectives, multi-level thinking. It requires maintaining a third-person perspective. It requires that we actively listen so we can understand both sides of the situation. It requires being aware of the problem we are addressing and the shifts in the quality of the relationship we share with the other person. It requires being aware of the process and criteria being used. It requires stepping back and being aware of our behavior and how our behavior is affecting the other person. It requires listening to our beliefs and assumptions, our feelings and our needs. It requires noticing when our capacities are constricted. It also requires paying attention to all these same factors in the other person.

Attending to the obvious requires using our capacities to focus and analyze, to see the differences. It also requires us to be insightful, to see the similarities between all the persons involved, to see the whole picture and to empathize with the other person's needs.

Attending to the obvious requires that we have one foot in and one foot out. We are in the midst of the process and at the same time we are stepping back, aware of various dynamics. *It is being an objective observer and being present at the same time.* It is

Figure 1.
Basic Questions For ATTENDING TO THE OBVIOUS

CONTENT	RELATION-SHIPS	NEEDS	PROCESS	CRITERIA
What are the issues? Do we need to take a broader viewpoint?	Are we on the same side of the table? Are they getting defensive?	What results do I need?	Is the process we are using working?	Do we have agreement?
Do we need to take a narrower view?	Do I trust them? Accept them? Resent them? What are they feeling toward me?	What results do they need?	Are we moving toward or away from resolution?	Do we have fair standards for settlement?

being authentically involved without losing yourself in the process. (See Figure 1.) We can only do this, we can only assume both positions effectively, while operating from Generative thinking. Only at this level can we use multi-perspective thinking and operate from more than one perspective at the same time.

HOW TO AVOID GETTING SEDUCED

In the midst of a negotiation, it is easy to get lost in the process or in our own emotions. When this occurs, we tend to give up our own boundaries. We begin to plan our defense rather than listening to the other person. We get seduced into protecting ourselves and trying to win rather than moving toward a mutually beneficial resolution.

We can avoid being seduced in this way if we will attend to the obvious—if, from moment to moment, we will consciously ask ourselves what is immediately, obviously going on. We will know what is going on if we listen to our bodies—especially the vulnerable feeling in our stomachs and chests. Our bodies always tell the truth. They don't lie. They will tell us what to focus on—if we will only listen instead of telling ourselves what we think "should" be going on.

For example:

If you're silent and refuse to participate, I need to ask what your silence means and point out that there will be no resolution if we don't talk.

If you keep rambling off the subject and I'm confused, I need to say, "We've gotten off the track and I'm confused. Let's get back to the issue." You may then have to search around a bit to determine what *the issue* is at this point.

THE CHINESE BOX APPROACH

Negotiations are often nested like chinese boxes, a negotiation within a negotiation within a negotiation. As pointed out, before we can ever get to the specific problem, the content of the negotiation, we must sometimes negotiate in order to negotiate. Our first task in negotiating an issue may be to negotiate how and when and where we will negotiate—the process. We may need to negotiate what is going on in our relationship—the conflict. We may need to agree on fair standards or criteria for resolving the issues.

We may also need to negotiate with ourselves. If we are avoiding approaching the other person, we need to resolve the blocks within us that are keeping us stuck. The point is that unless we attend to what is obvious, we may never get the opportunity to address the problem that needs to be solved.

HOW TO GET TO THE REAL ISSUES

But how do you identify the real issues that need to be addressed? It's simple.

Often, when people have a conflict, they will put forth a problem that is symptomatic rather than directly address the relationship. Focusing first on the problem is a safer way to point toward the conflict. For example, I may resent your attempts to undercut me in staff meetings, but I confront you on your late project.

Even when people do address the relationship directly, they often are not aware of the real underlying needs. Instead, they tend to confront triggering events or symptomatic behaviors. They will talk about the fact that the other person was late rather than express their own vulnerable feeling of not being valued or important.

Only gradually do we work down to the real issues—each person's underlying needs. We will do this more quickly and stay on track if we will attend to what is obviously occurring in the moment and consciously bring it into the open.

For example:

Steve is the general manager of a printing business owned by Ross. They have had a close and trusting relationship for several years. Steve has done an excellent job, and Ross has complete confidence in Steve and has delegated a significant measure of responsibility and authority to him.

The immediate problem is that Steve has received an unsolicited offer of backing from a local entrepreneur to start his own printing firm. Steve feels torn between his loyalty to Ross and this opportunity. Steve wants to take the new offer, but he also wants to be fair to Ross and maintain their relationship. Notice how Steve attends to what is immediately going on and, by doing so, moves from the initial problem to identifying the underlying issues.

Steve: I asked you to have lunch with me today because I have a problem I need to discuss with you.

Ross: Sure. What is it?

States initial problem:

Steve: I've been offered financial backing to start my own printing firm. I did not seek out the offer. It came as a surprise to me. I don't want to set myself up to compete with you here. If I take the offer, I will move to Silverdale.

Ross: Sounds like you've decided to do it.

Steve: Not definitely. We still have some details that need to be worked out. It is very appealing, though.

Ross: Well, there is no way that I can run this whole operation by myself and I don't have anyone to replace you. I thought you were committed to this company.

Focuses on relationship:

Steve: Wait a minute. I feel like I'm being emotionally blackmailed. I hear you jumping to catastrophic conclusions. I want to be fair to you, and I also want to be fair to myself. I appreciate all that you have done for me. I am committed to being fair to you and to helping you in any way I reasonably can. But I am not committed to being responsible for you—and that's what I hear you asking.

Ross: I don't know what you're talking about. I've never asked you to be responsible for me.

Focuses on immediate process:

Steve: Ross, let me backtrack for a minute. We are getting into a defensive fight rather than working together to solve our problem. Let me try to describe the whole picture that I see.

Ross: Alright, I guess.

Focuses on the problem:

Steve: The problem as I see it is not whether I decide to take this offer. The problem is whether your company is going to survive with or without me. I don't think I'm the determining factor. There are any number of qualified people who can do what I'm doing. If I decide to leave, I will not leave until we have someone in my place.

What concerns me is the financial stability of this company. We are still operating from hand to mouth. We don't have the financing we need to cover ourselves if we hit a thin period. It would take only two bad months and we would have a real crisis.

Ross: I'm doing what I can about that. I'm only one person.

Identifies the underlying need:

Steve: Your response highlights what I see as the real source of the problem. I don't think you really want the responsibility of running this firm. I think you feel overwhelmed by it and I think you believe you need someone else to take care of you. As a result, I think you are sabotaging the business.

Ross: You're crazy!

Focusing on the process:

Steve: Will you just listen to me and let me explain? Ross, I'm not trying to "get" you. I'm trying to solve our problem.

Ross: So, what makes you think I don't want to be responsible for myself?

Focuses on the causes:

Steve: I have several pieces of data. The first is that you spend a lot of time working, but you don't spend much time in the office doing the things that will really make a difference. I see you spending a lot of time talking to people and procrastinating doing the tough things—like firing the bookkeeper that needs to be fired. Second, we've talked more than once about our need to establish a line of credit. I can't do it, and you won't do it, and until we get a new bookkeeper, we do not have the data we need to get a line of credit. Third, the real drain on this business is your car collection. You're spending time and money on your antique cars that needs to be spent here if this business is going to survive. Fourth, I hear you wanting me to be responsible for you—to save your business. I can't. I can't save it even if I stay. Only you can do that.

Ross: Well, you're pretty convincing. (Silence)

Focuses on silence (process and underlying needs):

Steve: What are you thinking and feeling?
Ross: I'm not thinking about anything. I'm feeling confused and overwhelmed.
Steve: What do you need?
Ross: I'm not sure. I think I need some time to let this settle in. You're right about my procrastinating. I guess I have wanted you to save me. Seems like I've had to be responsible for myself all my life. If your offer works out, do what you need to do.
Steve: I won't leave until we have everything in place here. But I need you to take the time to fire the bookkeeper and to see about getting a line of credit. And I want you to think about the time and money you are spending on your cars.
Ross: I will. I'm not sure what to do about replacing you.
Steve: Do you want me to begin looking around?
Ross: Yes.
Steve: What are you feeling now?
Ross: I think it will all work out. I appreciate your honesty. I feel resolved with you.
Steve: Me, too. Thanks.

The skill of attending to what is obvious is described more fully in the chapters on the No-Fault Formula.

Key Points To Remember About Attending To the Obvious

- Avoid getting blocked.
- Avoid getting drawn into lower, nonproductive levels.
- Know when to shift focus from the problem to the relationship, the process, the criteria.

- Recognize when the other person is feeling threatened and you must create a safer environment.
- Remain on track. Don't be sidetracked by symptomatic issues and behaviors.
- Move toward addressing the real issues—the underlying needs of both persons.

Attending to the obvious is the single most important strategy in any negotiation. It will enable you to keep your power without unintentionally giving it away.

Chapters 4, 6, 8, and 10 specifically outline a wide range of strategies for successfully countering various blocking maneuvers. Attending to the obvious underlies all of these strategies. If we fail to attend to the obvious, we won't know what is going on and we will not choose appropriate strategies.

Considering all the possible strategies sometimes seems overwhelming. How can we remember what to do when? There's a simple answer. *Attend to the obvious.* If we attend to the obvious, we will naturally do what we need to do from moment to moment. We will reach resolution.

The only real failure in life is the failure to listen to what is true within us.

SECTION IV

THE PROCESS

CHAPTER 16

THE NO-FAULT FORMULA: FIVE EASY STEPS

IT'S MAGIC

The No-Fault Formula gets more of what you want, more often, from more people. Simple and effective, the No-Fault Formula provides a five-step process for:

1. Creating a safe environment.
2. Shifting your focus from problems to relationship conflicts, process, or criteria issues.
3. Creating mutual understanding instead of pitted battles.
4. Attending to the obvious.

The formula also helps you to avoid getting stuck in your negotiations. By using the Formula, you will recognize blocks as they arise. When you do get stuck, the Formula provides a means of moving the negotiation forward.

In short, it is the way to effectively implement everything presented in this book. You may not be able to create miracles, but this formula will provide a good bit of magic. IT WORKS.

More than just another quick trick (although it is that), it is a way of thinking. It is a way to stay clear and focused on the important issues. My experience, and the experience of many others who have learned to think in terms of these five steps, is a sharp increase in both the quality and the quantity of the results we want.

You'll be surprised how well it works. It's even easy. It just takes a little practice.

The Five Steps

The formula has five steps:

1. I See/Hear—THE DATA

Identify and describe, without judgment, the specific behavior or events which have occurred or are occurring. Be clear about what has been and is going on, or about the conditions that exist.

For example:

"I noticed you..."

"I hear you saying..."

"My data is..."

"The facts are..."

What facts do I have? What happened? What do we know about the situation? Do others have data that might be useful? What data do we need in order to understand the problem fully? What are they doing? Saying? What am I doing? Saying?

2. I Assume—INTERPRETING THE DATA

Identify and possibly share my assumptions or interpretations of the above events or behaviors. Search out possible causes for the problem or conflict. Why do I think these events are occurring? What am I saying to myself about the data?

For example:

"My assumptions about your behavior are..."

"It seems to me that... "

"I believe/am concluding that..."

"I think the reasons are..."

"I feel that this has occurred because..."

3. I Feel—THE COST OR IMPACT

The cost can be time, money, relationships, productivity, or emotions.

Describe what you are experiencing emotionally. Describe how the above events and behavior are affecting you and others. What is it costing you or the organization financially, or in terms of productivity, time, or use of resources?

For example:

"I am angry, frustrated, concerned, etc..."

"The client is feeling..."

"As a result, the other staff members are..."

"As a result, we lost the contract."

"As a result, we have missed our target date."

4. I Need—THE ALTERNATIVE DESIRED RESULTS OR CONDITIONS

The needs are what you want but are not currently getting.

Describe your internal needs or what you need that is different from what you are getting. Needs may be stated in terms of individual or organizational goals and objectives.

For example:

"My preference is to resolve this issue, meeting your needs and mine, if possible."

"I need to feel that my concerns are being heard."

"I need to have a contract I can take back and sell to my Board."

"Our objective in this situation is to..."

5. I Want/Will—THE PLAN OF ACTION

The 'WANTS' are what you want behaviorally from the other person in response to your needs. This is the proposed solution or answer. It is what you want others to do and what you are willing to do in order to create the results or conditions you need (Step 4). The plan of action always refers to behavior—WHAT WE ARE GOING TO DO.

For example:

"I want you to..."

"I want you to give me a report by Friday, and I will let you know then what I have found out."

"What I need from you is..."

"Will you go with me to the store?"

"I am willing to listen, and I need you to talk."

UNDERSTANDING THE FORMULA: WHY IT WORKS

STEP 1: I SEE/HEAR

How To Gather Your Data

In the first step of the Formula, you describe the specific behaviors, events, or conditions about which you are negotiating. This is an attempt to identify and clarify for yourself and for the other party the substantive/problem issues as well as the triggering events that tell you there is a problem. You may describe behaviors or events which have occurred in the past or which currently exist. You may also need to describe any environmental factors that are affecting the current situation. You describe your data—the data that tells you a problem or conflict exists. It means getting an overview of the situation.

The value of this step is that it gives you greater clarity about the context from which you are drawing your perceptions. It is the first step in beginning to define the issues. This step is also useful as a reality check. As you share the data you have with the other person, you are able to check whether you have all the facts. If you do not have all the facts, the other person probably will fill in with the additional pieces they have. Getting agreement about the facts is an essential first step in any negotiation.

Often it is useful to have two opposing parties in a negotiation gather data together so they have a common database. I have used combined labor/management or marketing/production committees to research and collect data prior to or during a negotiation.

How To Get To The Real Issues

Describing your data is how you implement the principle of Attending to the Obvious. You do it by paying attention to what is immediately, obviously going on before you and describing that data to the other party.

Observing and listening to what the other person is saying and doing during a negotiation gives us the immediate, ongoing data we need to move toward a successful resolution. Usually, what we begin talking about in a negotiation is not what we end up talking about. We often begin with symptoms and move toward clarifying the real issues. We clarify the real issues by paying attention to what is immediately going on before us and by identifying underlying needs.

Attending to the obvious also means being conscious about what we know—whether it is the past and current behavior of the other party or current environmental conditions. Again, only by consciously focusing on present reality, not on our fantasies, do we reach the real issues.

How To Clarify Double Messages

To stay with foreground, we actively listen to what the other person is saying and doing during the negotiation process. We feed back to them what we are observing and taking in. Active listening to foreground behavior is important because the other person often gives us incongruent or double messages. Active listening is a way to point out inconsistencies in what is said and done. It is a way to stay focused on the real issues and not be put off by the other person's denials and games.

Other Party: No, I'm not angry!

Your Response: I hear you say you're not angry, but your tone of voice and the look in your eyes tell me you are.

or

Other Party: No, I did not do it!

Your Response: I hear you say you didn't do it, but I also know that you were the only one in the office last night.

Attending to the other person's double messages alerts us to potential blocks as they arise. Paying attention makes us conscious of changes in our relationship with the other person, at the same time we are aware of the content of the discussion.

Make Them Accountable

This step provides us with a tool for being persistent. By feeding back the data we are receiving, we can consistently bring the data we have into the open. Thus, we are able to hold the other party accountable.

For example:

You may have a salesperson who promises results but does not get the job done. When you confront her, she says, "No problem, I can do it," in her best rah, rah! cheerleader voice. By attending to the obvious, you can point out that past experiences together with her tone of voice make you doubt that she will do it. You may need to repeat this several times until you can get her to address the underlying problems that are blocking her performance.

Create A Safe Environment

Describing our data by actively listening is a primary means by which we create safe environments. Active listening slows down the process of negotiating. For an extrovert, active listening means having the opportunity to think out loud. For introverts, it means having more time to process what is happening.

In addition, as the pace of a discussion speeds up, people become increasingly threatened and defensive. Taking the time to let them know that you heard them slows the pace 100 percent. Making them do the same slows the pace 200 percent and keeps both of you grounded in reality.

Active listening also helps create safe environments by allowing other people to know they are being accurately heard and understood. When other people feel understood, their capacities expand and they become less defensive.

Describe, Don't Judge

As we point out our data, it is important that we describe rather than judge. We need to be specific about our facts and avoid the temptation of making broad, sweeping generalizations. For example, "I've noticed we have gotten four complaints about the billings this month" is a nonjudgmental statement compared to "You always do a sloppy job on the billings." "They would not make a commitment during the meeting" is descriptive versus "They are resistive and stubborn."

STEP 2: I ASSUME

How To Interpret Your Data

In the second step of the formula, you let the other person know how you are interpreting the data. You share your assumptions and perceptions.

Sharing your assumptions is valuable for two reasons. First, it helps the other person understand you, what you are thinking and why. He is better able to understand and accept why you have responded behaviorally in certain ways. It helps him make sense of you.

Second, it allows you to check out the validity of your assumptions. One of the primary causes of unnecessary conflict in negotiations is false assumptions and failing to check them out. Checking out your assumptions is often one of the quickest ways your conflicts can get resolved.

I have a bittersweet example of this:

A client called me and complained bitterly because his partner had not shown up at the office for two days. He called me because I had been mediating some conflicts in their relationship. He assumed his partner was being passive-aggressive, and dumping everything on him to pay him back, and in his anger, he walked out to "even the score" and didn't come back for two days.

As it happened, my client's partner had been in an automobile accident and was in the hospital. In the family's concern and confusion, no one had thought to call my client, and he in turn had not bothered to call his partner to check out his assumptions. So much for false assumptions.

Distinguish Between Assumptions And Judgments

It is important to distinguish between sharing our assumptions and judging the other person. For example, we might have an employee who has arrived late at work. We might ask that employee if he came late because he is angry about the performance review he received the day before. Or, we might tell him we think he has a bad attitude (judgment). These are different types of statements. Sharing our assumptions encourages increased understanding. Judging other people constricts their capacities and encourages them to become defensive.

When sharing assumptions, we try to make specific statements about specific behaviors. The intent is to clarify the motives behind the other person's behavior or to understand why certain events have taken place. It is a step in defining further the causes for the conflict or problem.

In judging the other person, we tend to make broad, sweeping statements. The intent is to "beat" the other person, to get them to admit they are wrong, or to try to make them feel guilty. Judging is non-productive. It creates unnecessary blocks in the negotiating process.

Useful And Non-Useful Questions

One way to avoid making judgmental statements is to phrase our comments as tentative questions rather than as dogmatic truths. We check out our perceptions rather than condemning the other person.

If you do use questions to check out your assumptions, make sure they are factual questions. Avoid using rhetorical questions designed to make the other person admit he is wrong. Again, the purpose of checking out assumptions is to enhance understanding, not to make the other person more defensive. For example:

"I'm wondering..."

"When you do that, I assume..."

"Did you not call because you were angry?"

"Do you assume I'm not interested?"

Non-useful statements and questions:

"I think you deliberately did that to sabotage the meeting."

"When you do that, you make a fool out of yourself."

"How do you think I felt when you didn't call?"

"Do you think you're the only one interested in the outcome of this case?" (This is a judgment couched as a rhetorical question.)

"Why did you do that (Stupid)?" (This is another rhetorical question.)

As this last question illustrates, "Why" questions are usually sneaky judgments. Translate your "Why" questions to "What" and drop the superior dismissal and sarcasm from your voice, if you do not want want to come across as judgmental.

STEP 3: I FEEL

How To Clarify The Impact

In this third step, your intent is to help the other person understand how events or behaviors are affecting you, and possibly others, perhaps even the organization. Your purpose is to clarify the effect on yourself and others.

It is important that you make the other party feel your presence. Failure to make your presence felt encourages him to relate to you as an object rather than a real person. It allows him to avoid you, ignore you, deceive you, and dismiss you. *Other people need your help to bring you into focus.*

Good Negotiators Know What They Are Feeling

Sharing emotional impact is very important and often avoided. But being clear about what you are experiencing emotionally is important to you and the other person. It is important to you because getting clear about what you are specifically feeling tells us what you are specifically needing. This is particularly true of feelings of vulnerability.

Anytime we get angry, it is because we feel diminished or devalued as a person or because we are threatened. Our anger is our natural self-defense, an internal message that says we need to stand up for ourselves. Underneath our anger is always some feeling of vulnerability. We get angry because we are frightened or embarrassed or dismissed or misunderstood. If we listen to the feelings of vulnerability beneath our anger, they will tell us what we need.

If we are frightened, we need more safety or assurance. If we are embarrassed, we need more protection. If we are dismissed or misunderstood, we need to be taken seriously and be listened to.

Listening to our emotions is important because they tell us when we have a conflict which needs to be addressed. When we feel attacked or dismissed, when we feel as though we are fighting with the other person rather than dancing with them, we know we have a conflict as well as a problem.

Communicating what we are experiencing emotionally is important for us to be understood. Sharing our feelings with the other person gives him more personal data about us. If we want to be understood, we must be willing to let the other person know what we are feeling and what we are thinking.

Sharing our feelings invites other people to see us as a flesh and blood person like themselves. To share only what we are thinking invites other people to objectify us, to see us as different from them rather than like them. When we are sharing only our thoughts in a negotiation, the other person is more likely to perceive us as an object to be beaten rather than as a person to be understood.

By sharing what we are experiencing emotionally, we are more likely to see how we are alike and what we have in common. Sharing emotions moves both persons toward a cooperative relationship.

Our tendency is to avoid sharing our emotions. We find it easier to tell the other person what we are thinking, to share our opinions. Sharing our emotions is more personal and, therefore, more vulnerable.

Don't Confuse "I Feel" With "I Feel That"

We often give the appearance of sharing our emotions, when in reality we are judging the other person. This is evident when we use the term "I feel that..." or "I feel like..." followed by the pronoun "you."

"I feel that..." is not a statement of feelings. It is a statement of what we think. It is usually a sneaky way to judge the other person. Translated, "I feel that... " really means "I think you are wrong, stupid, selfish, misguided, etc." "I feel that you..." statements are about the other person, not our own experience.

Statements of our personal emotional experience are synonymous with the verb "to be." "I AM angry" (or overwhelmed or excited or frustrated) is a statement about us, not the other person. This is a subtle but important linguistic point. We often think we are sharing our experience and wonder why the other person is becoming constricted and defensive.

When we find the other person becoming defensive, we need to stop and get honest with ourselves. We need to verify whether we are really sharing our emotional experience to increase understanding and cooperation between us. Usually we are subtly trying to "beat" the other person, to point out to them how they are wrong. We do it in a sneaky way so they cannot come back on us.

Rule of Thumb: Eliminate such statements as "I feel that you. . ." and/or "I feel as if you. . ." from your negotiating vocabulary. They are rarely productive.

Organizational Impacts

In addition to personal or emotional impact, a situation often has organizational effects as well. Current events or conditions may be affecting whether the organization is:

- Fulfilling its mission.
- Living out of its values.
- Achieving its goals and objectives.
- Managing itself effectively.
- Creating a quality work environment.
- Making it in the marketplace.

To identify organizational effects, the following questions are helpful:

1. Is the organization fulfilling its stated mission? Are we doing what we are supposed to be doing?
2. Are we acting congruently with our espoused values? In what ways are we living up to our criteria for success? In what ways does our behavior contradict our values?
3. Are we achieving our goals and objectives? Are we on track and on time?
4. What effect is the current situation having on:
   - Our reporting relationships?
   - How we make decisions and solve problems?
   - The flow of information in all directions in the organization?
   - How people are being rewarded?
5. What effect is the current situation having on:
   - Individual productivity?
   - Individual attitudes?
   - Internal relationships?
   - The psychological climate. Is it positive? Cynical? Stressed? Overwhelmed? Trusting? Energetic? Resigned? Negative?
6. What effect is the current situation having on:

- Our relationships with our clients?
- Our share of the marketplace?
- Our relationships with our competitors?

These questions provide a framework for determining the impact of problems and conflicts on your organization.

Step 4: I Need

How To Identify Alternate Needs And Desired Outcomes

Needs are internal to people and organizations. Personally, they have to do with the quality of our physical and psychological existence. We need food and shelter and rest. We need to feel valuable and worthwhile. We need to feel adequate and capable. We need to feel as though we belong and that we are not alone. We need to make sense out of our lives. This is the stuff of any negotiation. We know what we need when we listen to what we are experiencing emotionally.

Organizationally, needs have to do with the effectiveness and efficiency of the organization in fulfilling its mission. It is what the organization needs to accomplish its business—its reason for existence.

If the purpose of all negotiation is to get other people to do what we want, to cooperate with us, then stating what we need is the heart of the negotiating process. This is the step which is most often skipped over. We seem to find it easier to tell others what we want them to do and how we want them to be different than to tell them what we need.

Again, the reason for this is that we are afraid of being too vulnerable. We are afraid of being taken advantage of if we let them know what we need, personally or organizationally.

Ironically, the whole purpose of negotiating is to meet individual or organizational needs. If we do not state what we need, we are not likely to get our needs met. To tell another person what we want from them without stating our underlying needs makes it difficult for them to understand us. They are much more likely to respond in the ways we desire when they understand why. To state what we need and why gives validity to our particular requests. It lets the other person know we are not making arbitrary demands.

And again, as I pointed out (in Chapter 14, *Understand Others, Don't Beat Them*), the *requirements that I need* are different from *my solutions*—what it is I want others to do to help me meet my needs.

Having made a case for stating our needs, let's add a word of caution. Sometimes it is foolish to tell the other person what we need when the other person is obviously out to take advantage of us. In these cases, we need to proceed more slowly. We need to use common sense about when we are unnecessarily giving ourselves away by being too open. We may need to get agreement about fair criteria for a settlement before stating our needs.

To tell a prospective employer that I desperately need the job and do not have any other offers is probably not to my best advantage. If our corporation is in serious financial trouble and everyone in top management is in survival mode, it is probably a fair assumption that the other drowning rats are not particularly concerned with my needs. If I know a buyer is trying to put the squeeze on me, I'm not going to tell him how badly I need to sell the property.

At the same time, most negotiating does not take place in Enforcer environments. More often, it will be to your advantage to make a clear presentation of your needs.

STEP 5: I WANT/WILL

How To Develop Your Plan Of Action

What we want in a negotiation is always some change in the external conditions or a change in the behaviors of the other person. What we want is what we perceive to be the solution to our problem or conflict.

People often have difficulty distinguishing between what they need FOR THEMSELVES and what they perceive as their best solutions—what they *want others* to do to help them meet their needs. Again, needs are the results, outcomes, or conditions necessary for our physical, fiscal, psychological, or relational existence. *Wants* (solutions) are what we want others to do to help us meet our needs. They are the ways we are both going to achieve our needs. Our needs and our wants (solutions) are separate but related realities.

I need to be treated fairly and I want (the solution) you to agree to fair criteria for settling my insurance claim.

I need to be respected by my staff, and I want (the solution) you to respect me by not confronting me in front of them.

I need to be understood and I want (the solution) you to listen to me and not walk away.

I need to get pressure off of me; therefore I want (the solution) you to get the project brought up-to-date.

I need to know my teenager is safe, and I want (the solution) her home by midnight.

Quite simply, the importance of stating what we want (the solution) is that:

1. We let the other person know clearly what it is we are asking from them behaviorally.
2. We clarify what must happen if we are to achieve our goals.

Negotiations often fail or are hampered because we do not state what we want. To tell someone I am angry with them or that I am disappointed in their performance without telling them specifically what I want them to do leaves them hanging. To tell you that I don't trust you and then not tell you what you could do so I would trust you is a Gotcha! I cannot expect others to read my mind. If I do expect that, I'm likely to be disappointed.

Eleven Benefits Of The No-Fault Formula

You can use the Formula for many purposes. It is a process to:

1. Keep you in Generative capacities for thinking so you can see the whole picture accurately without getting defensive.

2. Help you move the other party into Generative capacities and out of self-protective behavior.
3. Identify what the real issues are that need to be addressed.
4. Stay on track and not get off on tangents.
5. Prepare for negotiations before you move into them—to lay out your strategy.
6. Expand your capacities for empathy so you accurately understand the needs of the other party.
7. Analyze conflicts, performance problems, or organizational problems.
8. Confront others about their behavior—including performance problems.
9. Improve your listening skills.
10. Clarify your internal needs.
11. Develop plans of action to solve personnel or organizational problems.

THE FIVE STEPS ILLUSTRATED

The following example illustrates using the five steps as an analytical tool:

I see/hear

I'm aware that Martha is shifting in her chair. Her voice sounds tentative, and she is avoiding eye contact. I also know she has been having problems with her staff. They are frustrated because she has procrastinated confronting her division manager about his performance.

I assume

I'm assuming she is not comfortable with what I am proposing to do in the staff retreat. I think she is afraid that she will be confronted publicly by some of her staff members.

I feel

I feel concerned that she may veto the retreat or dilute the process so that nothing significant happens.

I need

I need to find a way to help her feel safe with the process and to trust me.

I want/will

I want her (the solution) to tell me what she is feeling and thinking right now. I want to understand her specific fears so we can create a process that will be non-threatening and effective. I want her to tell me what she needs to be able to trust me.

In this example, I have both a problem and a conflict to address. You will find more examples of the different uses of the Formula in the next chapter.

CHAPTER 17

THREE USES OF THE FORMULA

As outlined at the end of Chapter 16, the Formula has many uses. Overall, it is useful as an analytical tool, a confrontational tool, and as an ongoing negotiation tool.

AN ANALYTICAL TOOL

HOW TO GET CLEAR ABOUT YOUR PROBLEMS AND NEEDS

First, the No-Fault Formula can be used as an analytical tool to clarify what our issues are in a situation we need to address. Going through the steps in the Formula is a quick and simple way to identify our problem and conflict issues, or to analyze performance and organizational problems.

It is an effective means of preparing for a negotiation session—to get clear about what we are needing and what we want as an outcome of the negotiations. Using the Formula is a way to clarify whether we need to focus on the problem, the relationship, the process, or the criteria.

HOW TO ANALYZE A CONFLICT

The Formula is a quick and easy way to get clear about where you are in relation to another person. By going through the steps, you will gain clarity about:

- What is going on in you.
- What the other person is doing to produce those effects in you.
- What you need or what is unresolved for you with the other person.
- What you want them to do (solution) in order for you to achieve resolution.

For example:

I SEE—My Data: John didn't talk to me or acknowledge me when I came in the office this morning. I just heard him say that he doesn't trust that I am authentic, that I am who I appear to be. Last week, he challenged the validity of my analysis of the problem in the factory. He said I was too glib.

I ASSUME—My Interpretation: I assume his comments only partially have to do with me. I know (more data) that he distrusts consultants in general. I'm wondering if he is angry because I did not include him in the briefing with the president last week. I also have a sense that John and I operate on different clocks or at different speeds. I wonder if my fast reactions make him doubt the validity of my conclusions.

I FEEL—The Impact: I feel resentful about being ignored by him and I dislike his accusations or insinuations. I'm aware that others in the room are quiet and seem to feel uncomfortable, as if they're waiting for the storm to break. We obviously can't continue our meeting until we address our conflict.

I NEED—Different Results: I need to stay as non-defensive as possible and try to really understand what is prompting his comments. I need to have the tension in the room resolved. I need my relationship with John resolved so we can work together.

I WANT/WILL—My Plan of Action: I'm going to check out whether John is comfortable addressing our conflict in front of these other people. If not, I'm going to ask that this meeting be postponed until tomorrow and spend the time now with John trying to reach some mutual understanding.

To carry out this next step, now that I have some insight into what the issues are between John and myself, I decide to adjourn the meeting to talk to him about it. Watch how each of us drops into different styles of thinking and how the Formula enables us to get back to cooperative, Generative thinking. This is an example of using the Formula as a verbal negotiating tool.

I: *(I need)*	John, I want to try this morning to resolve what's going on between us. (Generative)
John:	I don't want to talk about it. It's a waste of time. (Enforcer Avoiding behavior)
I: *(I hear)*	John, I know that you are angry with me and don't trust me right now. (Generative side-stepping of his avoidance by responding to the real message that I heard.)
(I assume)	And I think you have good reason to feel the way you do. I believe I have done some things that upstaged you. (Creating a safer environment by acknowledging my own behavior.)
(I feel)	I'm feeling frustrated that we seem to go round and round and can't get our relationship on solid ground.
(I need)	The fact is we need to be able to work together and I'd like to be able to work with you without all the distrust and tension.
John: *(I need)* *(I feel)* *(I assume)*	I'd like to get this cleared up too. This hassling back and forth wears me out. But I still don't trust you and I don't know that we can work it out today. It's going to take time before I know whether I can trust you. (Scorekeeper Waiting behavior.) (Now, if I were to respond to this from a Generative posture, I'd confront his behavior and ask for a fuller explanation of his data and assumptions. However, not always being so Generative myself, I go on the attack.)
I: *(Formula temporarily aborted)*	You tick me off. Who do you think you are sitting in judgment of me? (Rebel Producer, dismissing with rhetorical question.) I resent it and I don't deserve it. (Scorekeeping.) I've done a lot of good work for you and you're too stupid to appreciate it. (It doesn't take me long to get right down on the Enforcer level.)

John: *(Ditto)* I can't help it if you perceive it as judging. I don't know if I can trust what you say. You always seem to have fast, easy answers, and I think you are very political. You give a lot of attention to department heads but you think you're too good to spend time with other people. (While the words sound like Rebel Producer dismissal, the resentment in his voice tells me that he is in Scorekeeper thinking.)

I: *(I hear)* (Pause) You sound resentful. (Almost Generative)

John: *(I feel) (implied I need)* I guess I am but I'm not sure why. I'm not very comfortable with your anger, and I'm not sure we are getting much resolved. (Generative)

I: *(I feel) (I assume) (I need)* I'm aware that I just want to blame you right now and get you to admit you're wrong. And I wonder if you want to do the same to me. I wonder if we can't get back on track here and try to understand what the real issues are between us. (Generative)

John: *(I feel)* I'm willing. If I were to be totally honest, I'd say I resent you coming in here and getting all the attention when I am the one who's here day in and day out doing all the unglamorous work. And I'm also jealous of your friendship with Lloyd—and I'm embarrassed to tell you that. (Generative)

I: *(I see) (I feel) (Implied I need)* Thank you for your honesty. For my part, I think in my need to have everyone think I'm wonderful I need to hog the spotlight. And I'm embarrassed that is still true about me. I'm sorry that I was so engrossed with making a good presentation to the president that I didn't give you credit or an opening to say much. (Generative)

John: *(I want) (I feel) (I need)* Thank you. (Pause) What are your feelings now? (Generative)

I: Relieved and resolved and wondering where your trust level is with me. (Generative)

John: I feel resolved. Let's get back to work.

How To Expand Your Capacity For Insight And Empathy

In addition to using the Formula to get clear about what is going on in us, we can also use it to expand our insight and empathy into others. To do so, we go through the same five steps, only this time from the other person's perspective:

- What data do they have?
- How are they interpreting that data?
- What impact is my behavior and/or the events having on them?
- What do they need?
- What do they want me to do?

To follow through with the example with John:

His Data: I failed to reschedule my briefing with the president so he could attend. I frequently talk a lot and with great authority.

His Interpretation: He probably wonders about my authenticity or sincerity since I failed to include him in the briefing. He probably questions the validity of my analyses when I present them so quickly and casually.

His Impact: He probably doesn't feel respected or valued by me. He may feel run over by me in meetings. He certainly doesn't feel very trusting toward me right now.

His Need: He probably needs to understand my intentions, to understand why I didn't reschedule the briefing with the president. (I honestly forgot because I was on vacation the week before.) He probably also needs me to explain how I arrived at my conclusions.

His Wants/Will: He probably wants (solution) me to adjourn the meeting so we can talk in private.

How To Analyze And Solve Performance Problems

We can also use the Formula to analyze and address performance problems. Nonperformance is always caused by one or more of the following factors:

1. Lack of skill or knowledge.
2. Organizational or environmental blocks.
3. Relationship conflicts.
4. Personal problems that result in self-protective behaviors.

To use the formula to analyze a performance problem:

1. *State Your Data:* Write a description of the current behavior that is not acceptable, e.g., the sales manager acts confused and indecisive. He doesn't prioritize his decisions, he comes to me for help with simple decisions, and he procrastinates making important decisions.
2. *Interpret Your Data:* List what you think the causes are for the above behavior you've listed, using the four factors identified above as a framework. For example:
    1. I assume after being in this business for twenty years that he has the necessary skills and knowledge to carry out his job.
    2. I think his recent marriage may be taking up a lot of his attention.
    3. I think our organization's lack of a decision-making matrix which clearly delineates decision-making authority is probably causing him some confusion.
    4. I think he is afraid of me because of my impatient manner and he probably is worried about not having my approval.
    5. I have also noticed that when he gets tense or scared, he gets confused. I think part of the prob-

lem is a nonproductive behavior pattern he has for dealing with stress.

3. *Assess The Impact:* What's the impact on you, others, and the organization? What's it costing you? For example, all the other senior managers are frustrated because his indecisiveness is making it difficult for them to get their jobs done. They have all come to me and complained, and now I'm worried about whether he can really do the job. I'm feeling irritated and losing my confidence in him.
4. *Define The Need:* Define the different performance requirements and/or outcomes you need. For example, I need him to complete a marketing plan by November. I need him to start prioritizing his decisions, to stop procrastinating, and to start making decisions about the reorganization of his staff and our sales strategy, and I need him to stop coming to me to make his decisions for him. (NOTE: Using the Formula to *analyze* performance problems is one time when the NEED can also be a *behavior*—the behavior in this instance is part of the desired outcome.)
5. *Plan Your Action:* Outline what you need to do to get a change in his behavior. For example, I'm going to make a decision-making matrix for the sales department. I'm then going to sit down with him and go through my analysis of the problem and make it very clear to him what I need and what I want him (solution) to do. I'm going to give him a specific assignment to use this Formula to analyze his staffing and sales needs and to come back to me in a week with a plan of action—proposed solutions. I'm also going to check out if he is feeling intimidated by me and what he would need from me to feel more at ease. I'm going to suggest that he meet with our management consultant to understand and eliminate his pattern of confusion. And if all this doesn't bring about the necessary results in two months, I'm going to replace him.

How To Analyze And Solve Organizational Problems

In addition to analyzing personal conflicts and performance problems, we can also use the Formula to analyze and address organizational problems.

1. *State Your Data:* Write a description of the problem. We have lost 3 percent of our market share in the past two months. State your other related data. For example, we have a new general manager. Decisions are taking longer to get made. I've noticed people standing around the coffee pot complaining about the pressure they feel. We recently went through a reorganization.
2. *Interpret Your Data:* List what you think may be contributing to the problem. For example, I think the increased competition in the marketplace is a contributing factor. I also think the new general manager's style of wanting more decisions to go through him is causing decisions to be pushed up and is causing a bottleneck. I believe some people are unhappy about the reorganization and may be slacking off. And I believe that the new work-group alignments caused by the reorganization are causing some discomfort. People don't know each other well enough to trust each other and work together smoothly.
3. *Assess The Impact:* Define the impact on you, others, and the organization. For example, I'm feeling concerned and frustrated. Others apparently are also frustrated. We have lost the market share.
4. *Define The Need:* Describe what needs to be different in the organization—in its results and how it functions. For example, we need to gain back our market share. We also need to increase our productivity and have more effective work teams. We need to speed up decision-making and get more decisions moved down to appropriate levels in the organization. And we need to improve the work climate and reduce the stress our employees are feeling.

5. *The Plan of Action:* What are you going to do and what do you want others to do to achieve the necessary results? For example, I'm going to meet with my managers and check out my perceptions. Then I'm going to meet with the general manager and lay out my analysis and ask for his support in moving more decisions down the company ladder. I'm going to ask the marketing department to do an analysis of the changes in the marketplace. I am also going to ask our human resource department to do some coaching with any employees who seem to be disgruntled and dragging their feet. And finally, I'm going to schedule some team-building sessions for some of the new work groups who seem to be having problems.

A CONFRONTATIONAL TOOL

HOW TO USE THE FORMULA FOR GROUP PROBLEM-SOLVING

The Formula can be used not only by you individually to analyze personnel or organizational problems, it can also be used as a group process in any type of meeting. Frequently when I am working with companies, we put the five steps of the Formula (Data, Assumptions, Impact, Objectives/Needs, Plan of Action) on newsprint or a chalk board and then as a group brainstorm to fill in the categories.

This is an invaluable tool for group problem-solving. It helps a group stay focused so it doesn't wander off on tangents. It keeps individuals in the group in Generative thinking, non-defensive and problem-oriented, instead of personalizing the problem. And it helps the group discipline itself to define the problem before jumping to solutions.

HOW TO CONFRONT OTHERS WITH EASE

In addition to using the Formula to analyze problems and conflicts, the Formula is also useful when we need to be assertive and confront someone. Confrontation is necessary and appropriate when we do not have the time to negotiate or when we perceive the other person is not disposed to negotiate with us. We confront when we need something done in a hurry or when we need to get the other person's attention. When using the Formula to confront, we simply go through the elements once, being very specific and firm about what it is we want, about what solutions will be acceptable to us. The Formula is an effective way to draw our boundaries.

For example:

1. I see/hear–I have conclusive data that proves you have not been ringing up all your sales and have been pocketing the money.
2. I assume– I don't know what your motivation is for stealing the money but I cannot tolerate that behavior from an employee.
3. I feel– I'm angry and disappointed about this whole matter. I feel betrayed and used and I don't enjoy having to confront you about it.
4. I need–I need the stealing stopped immediately.
5. I want–Here's your final check. I am terminating you. I want you to clean out your locker and be gone within a half hour.

A Negotiating Tool

How To Negotiate Satisfactory Solutions

In addition to all the other wonderful uses of the Formula, it also provides a framework for ongoing negotiating. To use the Formula for negotiating, we simply keep going through the steps. The process is one of sending a whole, specific message to the other person by including all five of the elements in the Formula. Then we listen to their response. Their response is the new foreground data and it becomes our new Step One–what we see and hear. We reflect what we are observing and hearing, share our assumptions about that, and so on. The other person responds, and we repeat the process over and over, until we reach our desired resolution. The following example illustrates this.

Jeff: *(I need)*	Allen, I have a problem and I need your help with it.
Allen:	Sure, Jeff, what is it?
Jeff: *(I see/hear)*	It has to do with Marty. Since he is reporting to both of us, I have some confusion about how his time is supposed to be allocated. As you know, I requested his reassignment from your department to mine because the research on our report is due in four weeks.
(I assume)	I thought he would be working for me full-time,
(I see/hear)	but in the past week, he has been working for you three days.
(I assume)	I thought we had a clear understanding and that you had fully agreed with it.
(I feel)	I'm feeling really frustrated and pressured.
(I need)	I need to know when I can count on him being there.
(I want/will)	I guess I need some information from you on what your understanding is and what you are willing to agree to do.
Allen: *(I assume)*	My understanding when I agreed to let Marty go for the month was that I could call him back whenever I really needed him.
(I see/hear)	You know I'm in the process of converting the accounting systems in all of the branches.
(I need)	When more than one location breaks down, I have to have someone else to help me troubleshoot.
(I feel)	Frankly, I've been a little irritated about the whole situation. I never wanted to let him go in the first place.

Jeff: *(recycle)*	I hear the irritation in your voice.
(I see/hear)	I believe you when you say that that was your
(I assume)	understanding. For some reason, I understood it differently.
(I need)	I'm not clear what your irritation is about—I need to know whether you're simply irritated at the inconvenience or angry with me for requesting his transfer.
Allen:	It is inconvenient, but I'm primarily irritated at
(I feel)	the way it was done.
(I see/hear)	No one informed me of the change, let alone asked me, until two days before it took effect.
(I feel)	I don't like not having a voice in the matter. It's clear I don't have much authority here.

(Allen just dropped to resentful Scorekeeping thinking with this last little 'Gotcha' job. Jeff will now pull him back up to Generative thinking by giving Allen more data.)

Jeff:	Wait a minute. I think we have some crossed
(I assume)	wires here. I didn't call you personally and talk about it because I was in St. Louis when the decision was made.
(I see/hear)	Art said he had talked it over with you and assured me that it was agreeable with you. That was two weeks before Marty started working for me.
(I feel)	I feel embarrassed that I didn't call you myself to double check. (A shift to focusing on the relationship.)
(I need)	I need you to believe that I had no intention of overriding your authority. I have really valued our relationship. You've been very helpful to me and my department. I don't want to screw up our relationship.
Allen:	I believe you. I've valued the cooperation be-
(I need)	tween us in the past.
(I feel)	That's why I was surprised when this happened.

(Conflict is resolved.)

Jeff: *(I want/will)*	What do we need to do to solve the situation with Marty?

(Shift back to solving the problem.)

Allen: *(I want/will)*	What do you suggest?
Jeff: *(I need)*	Actually, I don't have to have him all the time but I do need him four days a week. And I need to know what days he's going to be here.
Allen: *(I need)*	Well, if I knew I had him one day a week, I could set up a schedule that would allow me to service the branches more efficiently and we wouldn't be having these emergencies.
Jeff: *(I need)*	Sounds good to me. I need to check whether you're OK with our relationship.
(I hear)	I heard some hesitation in your voice when you said "I believe you."

(Problem-solving)

Allen:	I feel resolved. Next time we have any questions, we need to talk to each other directly.
Jeff:	I agree. Thanks.

Key Points To Remember About The Formula

1. The Formula is a quick and simple way to define the issues you need to address. You can use it to prepare and plan for a negotiation.
2. It will help you clarify whether you have a relationship conflict as well as a problem to address.
3. It will help you focus on whether you need to address the process and criteria before addressing the problem.
4. It will help you gain insight into the other party, to recognize what their style of thinking is, and what they need to cooperate with you.
5. You can use the Formula to help you solve performance problems and organizational problems.

6. It works individually or as a group, problem-solving process.
7. It helps you to confront others with greater clarity and ease.
8. The Formula serves as a verbal guideline during the negotiation process.

The next chapter will provide you with helpful guidelines for putting the Formula into practice as a verbal framework for negotiating.

CHAPTER 18

USING THE FORMULA AS A VERBAL TOOL

RULES TO REMEMBER

This chapter outlines five key rules and seven behavioral factors that will help you effectively use the Formula as a verbal tool. The five key rules are:

1. Any Order.
2. A Guide for Whole.
3. Specific Statements.
4. Only One Person Needs to Know the Formula.
5. Talk About Us, Listen To Them.
6. Chosen Vulnerability.

1. ANY ORDER

The Formula is listed in a logical sequence of steps, but being logical is not always the highest criteria for effective communication. The formula may be used in any order, *with one exception*.

Never begin with step five, the solution. Beginning with what you want a person to do is likely to put him on the defensive. He may hear what you want as a demand or an unjustified request. To lead off with your proposed solutions or answers invites the other person to adopt an opposing solution which he then feels required to defend.

You want to build a case for your proposed solutions before stating them. More importantly, you'll be developing the solution together as you listen to and explore each other's needs. You want the other person to be engaged in his capacity for empathy. You want him to understand your experience and to feel the validity of your needs and interests. You want him in a posture of cooperation rather than one of defensive competitiveness.

One of the most effective ways to move the other person into a posture of cooperation is to begin with what we are feeling or needing. This is especially true if the other person is feeling defensive or threatened. To begin with what we need sets the norm for being vulnerable and honest. To begin with our needs invites the other person to move in closer. To begin with what we want pushes the other person away.

Which statement would make you feel more like cooperating?

I want the job done and I want it done now.

or

I'm feeling a lot of pressure. I have three people on my back wanting this report today. I need you to drop what you're doing and focus all your attention on getting this report finished as soon as possible.

The other person is going to be more receptive to listening to what else we have to say, if we begin by choosing to be vulnerable. The other person is much more likely to listen to us when we tell him we have a problem we need to solve and we want his help, than if we lead off by telling him we want him to come in on Saturday to work. Tell him that you want him to work on Saturday first, and he won't hear the rest of your statements. He'll be planning his defense.

When using the Formula, another dynamic frequently occurs: both parties focus on a single element at a time until each person has mutual clarity, then they move on to the other elements. For example, we may need to get the facts clear about what happened (Step 1), or clarify our assumptions about each other's behavior (Step 2). By clarifying the facts or our assumptions, we may find it unnecessary to go through the other steps.

So, use the Formula in any messy way you need to use it. Just use it.

2. A Guide For Whole, Specific Statements

The Formula should be used as a guide rather than as a rigid procedure. If we include all the steps, we are more likely to send a whole, specific message. One of the major blocks to successful negotiating is the fact that people tend to communicate with incomplete and generalized messages, leaving other people to fill in the gaps and inviting them to make false assumptions and to misunderstand.

Sometimes we do not need to include all the steps of the Formula because they are obvious to the other person. Sometimes, as in business negotiations, it may be inappropriate to share deeply what we are feeling. As a strategy, we may choose to not include one of the steps or we may choose to include it only partially—by letting them know, for instance, what impact they are having on us.

For example:

If I am negotiating a contract, I may not tell the other party specifically what I want. It would be to my disadvantage to tell her the price for which I would be willing to settle. I want to leave the situation open so she can make an offer.

In the same manner, it may be counterproductive to share all my assumptions about the other person's behavior. I may believe that he is stealing money from the company. It would be foolish for me to tell him my assumptions until I have the evidence I need to fire him without risk of a lawsuit or a protest from his union.

Sharing all our assumptions can also be counterproductive if by doing so we make the other person more defensive. Again, we need to use common sense about how much to share and when to share it.

3. Only One Person Needs To Know The Formula

Obviously, it is easier to negotiate if both parties know the Formula and communicate in whole, specific, nonjudgmental messages, but it is not essential. *What is essential is that we know the Formula.*

As we communicate in whole, specific messages, the other person is more likely to respond in the same way. As we share our assumptions and experiences and needs, rather than judge the other person, he is going to feel less defensive and will be more willing to let us know what is going on inside. As we actively listen so he feels understood, he will be more disposed to listen to us.

The Formula gives us a framework within which to listen more accurately. If, as often occurs, we do not receive whole or specific messages, we can ask for the missing pieces. We can ask the other person what they heard us saying (Step 1), or we can ask her what her assumptions are. We can ask what are the needs behind her demands, how she arrived at her position.

For example:

If the other party says he is angry, I can ask what made him angry and what he wants me to do in response. If he says he won't do something, instead of getting in a pitched battle by telling him he "should" do it or "will" do it, I ask what has made him adopt this position. If he says he can't do it, I ask him what he would need to be able to do it. If he wants me to do something that I don't want to do or that doesn't make sense to me, I can ask him how it will affect him (what the impact will be) if I do or don't do what he wants.

4. Talk About Us, Listen To Them

We know that we are using the formula correctly when we are focused on talking about ourselves and on listening to the other person. We know we are not using the Formula when we find ourselves not listening while we are planning our own reply. We know we are not using the Formula when we are judging the other person rather than being descriptive about the data and our experience. The underlying principle when we are negotiating is that we need to talk about ourselves, not the other person.

5. Chosen Vulnerability

Our greatest power lies in our chosen vulnerability. This does not mean we always tell all to everyone. It does mean people are more like us than different from us. It does mean that people do not usually live up to our worst fears.

For the most part, power is not something others take away from us; rather, we give our power away. We give it away every time we believe we need to hide—to hide who we are, what we are experiencing, and what we need. Every time I hide, I am saying to myself that I cannot trust the other person because I cannot trust myself.

We give our power away:

1. When we believe we have worth and value only if the other person approves of us.
2. When we believe the other person is smarter, more competent, or stronger.
3. When we believe others are more clever and can take advantage of us.
4. When we avoid confronting others because we are afraid we cannot protect ourselves from their response.
5. When we remain passive or confused because we are afraid of our own anger and power.

We affirm our power every time we decide to trust ourselves, to affirm ourselves. *We affirm our power every time we accept the fact that, in our limitedness, we are more than enough.*

When we believe in ourselves, we empower ourselves. When we accept ourselves, we have less need for the acceptance of others. When we believe we are worthwhile, we come out of hiding and go for 100 percent of what we want rather than settle for less. When we trust ourselves, we can afford to stand out, to be specific and clear, to make direct contact. When we trust ourselves, we can afford to be transparent, thereby creating a safer environment which invites the other person to move toward resolution rather than self-defense. When we trust ourselves, we can afford to listen to the other person, to take them in so they feel understood. This in turn makes it easier for them to listen to and understand us.

The power we get from hiding and planning our strategies does not match the superior power that comes from trusting ourselves and choosing to be vulnerable. The Formula gives us a structure within which we can realistically choose to be vulnerable. As you saw in the last chapter's example, the whole tone of the negotiation changed when John chose to be vulnerable by showing his jealousy of me.

Behavioral Factors—How To Effectively Use The Formula

Several behavioral factors may affect your degree of effectiveness in using the Formula. The following is a checklist.

1. **Voice Tone:** Often, more is communicated by our tone of voice than by the actual words we use. We can say "What do you want?" in many different tones. Depending on our tone of voice, those words may communicate threat, seduction, accommodation, dismissal, or acceptance.

In general, loud tones of voice have the advantage of getting attention and making a definitive point. Loud tones also have the effect of pushing others away and threatening them. Quiet or soft tones of voice tend to draw others in. Quiet tones literally make others lean forward and invite them to relax and feel safer. At the same time, quiet tones of voice may invite others to ignore you or take you less seriously.

Use your tone of voice to your advantage. Be firm when you need to be; gentle, warm, and inviting when you want to establish better rapport. And be congruent (words and tone matching) when you want to build trust.

Be aware that you can use your tone of voice to interrupt or break another person's nonproductive behavior pattern. By shifting your tone of voice, you may invite a different response and you can surprise the other parties. If they expect you to make a loud and angry response to their attack, surprise them by responding in a quiet, firm voice. You may be surprised at how powerful a tool your voice tone can be.

2. **Body Movement:** Your entire body is a visual environment. You communicate with your whole body. Get firmly planted on both feet with one hand on your hip and the other hand pointing if you want to exhibit strength and make a point. Lean back in relaxed repose if you want to send an invitation to come closer and feel safe. Shift your physical space for emphasis. If you want to make three points, move three times.

Use arm and hand movements to mark a distinction between separate ideas. Point up if you want your audience to see your point of view. Make a broad sweeping motion above eye level if you want them to see the whole picture. Put your hand by your ear if you want them to hear you. Make a gesture toward the trunk of your body when you want them to understand what is going on inside you.

Whole body movements are also useful when you get stuck. Changing your physical posture or position helps you change your perspective so stand up, sit down, walk around, exchange chairs, or move to the same side of the table as the other person.

3. **Breathing:** We pace one another unconsciously with our breathing. If you want to establish rapport, match the other person's breathing. If you want to speed up the conversation, just match their breathing, then start breathing faster. If you want to slow down the conversation, take some deep breaths, sigh subtly, and slow down your breathing. If you are not too obvious about it, you can effectively lead the other person to unconsciously speed up or slow down her rate of speaking by simply shifting your own rate of breathing. The same effect can be achieved by slowing down or speeding up the tempo of your rate of speaking.

4. **Matching Predicates:** Almost everyone uses a favorite sensory track to represent their experience. You can identify a

person's favorite sensory track by paying attention to the types of predicates he uses. Some people use primarily visual predicates ("It seems clear to me." "I see your point.") Others use primarily auditory predicates ("I can hear what you are saying." "It sounds like you have thought about it.") Others use primarily kinesthetic predicates ("I'm still trying to get a handle on what you said." "I can't quite grasp it yet.")

You can help establish rapport with others by using similar predicates. By using similar predicates you create congruence because others feel they are better understood. (Now, I hope that in light of what I have said, this will ring a bell and you will come to grips with how you are using language in your negotiations.)

5. **Wondering:** Two classes of people wonder—young children and wise adults. Wondering is primary to the learning process within each of us. If we never wonder, we never learn. We stay locked within outdated models of the world. Wondering, on the other hand, expands our options by allowing us to attain different points of view.

Wondering is a respectful and effective means of making a point with another person without making him or her defensive. It is a means of inviting others to join us in being curious. So, if you are deadlocked, invite him or her to wonder with you. "I wonder what would happen if we stopped blaming each other and started listening to each other?"

The invitation to wonder is one way of helping the other person to shift his or her focus or frame of reference. Rather than talk about whatever the content or problem is, invite the other person to wonder about the process—what we are behaviorally doing in the moment that is keeping us blocked.

The invitation to wonder immediately makes an ally of the other person. Rather than staying on opposite sides of the table and arguing about the problem, the two of us suddenly shift to the same side of the table, working together to identify the specifics of the process in which we are participating.

6. **Eye Movements:** You may have noticed that people move their eyes around a lot while they are talking. They tend to look up when they are expressing internal images, look levelly

when they are expressing internal sounds, and look down when they are expressing emotions.

We usually communicate a great deal with our eyes. Our eyes may snap or flare when we are angry, become half-masked when we are seductive, squint when we don't see the point, shift back and forth when we are frightened and looking for a way out, become unfocused or staring when we are confused, become downcast when we are embarrassed or unsure of ourselves.

Be aware of what you are communicating with your eyes. You may be giving away your power or pushing the other person away with your eyes. Look him straight in the eye if you want to communicate confidence. Get a playful glint in your eye if you want to break the tension. Draw him in with a gentle, silent, holding stare if you don't want him to get away from you.

7. Using Stories and Metaphors: Stories and metaphors are powerful tools. Telling stories or metaphors rather than directly making your point has a number of advantages, one of which is accessing the unconscious mind and resources of the other person. If the stories or metaphors contain visual, auditory, and kinesthetic elements, they speak to the whole person. The other person is much more likely to understand and experience what you want to communicate.

As children, we have all enjoyed hearing stories. As adults we still enjoy it. Telling stories has a tendency to relax the other person. In turn, he or she feels safer and is able to expand his or her cognitive capacities.

When you use metaphors, follow these three steps:

1. Decide on the desired outcome—what you want to achieve by telling the story.
2. Tell the story.
3. Do not explicitly tell the moral or point of the story. Invite the other person into the process and allow her to apply the story to her own experience.

Stories are useful in explicit and informal negotiation situations. An example of an informal occasion is when I am conducting seminars. If I am conducting a negotiation seminar with a work-related group in which competition, low trust, and fear of looking stupid are present, I will frequently begin the seminar by telling stories.

I may have the listeners close their eyes and relax. Then I tell a series of brief stories with which they can identify their own experience. I may talk about a time when, as a child, I moved into a new neighborhood and joined the neighborhood Kick-the-Can game. Or I may tell about times in my life when cooperation paid off, or times when I discovered other people were just as afraid of looking foolish as I was.

Then I invite my listeners to wonder about what they would need to feel safe, comfortable, and belonging in this particular learning group. When they open their eyes, I ask them to share what they are thinking about and what they need to maximize their experience in the seminar.

Through the process of telling stories, I have begun the negotiation by addressing their seminar needs. I have taken them through the internal steps of the Formula, allowing them time to reflect and relax in a safe manner.

Key Points To Remember About Using The No-Fault Negotiating Formula

1. It doesn't matter what order you use the Formula, as long as you don't start with the fifth step, the Solution.
2. Use the Formula as a guide for sending and receiving whole, specific messages.
3. Don't use the invalid excuse that you can't get what you want from someone because they don't know how to negotiate. *If you use the Formula, they have to use it also.*
4. Stay clear that your focus is to explain yourself so it is easy for them to understand you. Don't use the Formula to subtly "get" them.
5. *Be accountable* for your own contribution to what isn't working.

6. Use your voice tone, body movements, eye movements, breathing, and predicates to get the results you want.
7. *Wonder.*
8. Learn to be a good story-teller.

SECTION V

WHAT TO DO ON MONDAY MORNING

CHAPTER 19

KEY IDEAS

Now that you've absorbed all these concepts and principles and applied all these tools, what are you going to do with it all? How are you going to use the material to get more of what you want?

Just in case you don't have the book memorized and don't feel adept at using the tools, let me summarize the key points and make a suggestion or two for how to begin implementing these tools.

REVIEW OF NO-FAULT NEGOTIATING

We negotiate everyday in everything we do.

No-fault Negotiating is a process of creating mutual understanding to get others to cooperate with you in meeting your needs, while maintaining ongoing relationships.

The core premise is that *facing reality* will get you more of what you want, more often, from more people. Facing reality means:

- Accepting that you have a right to what you need, believe you can get it, and go for it 100 percent.
- Accepting the reality of who other people are and what they need to be able to cooperate with you.
- Accepting the real limitations of the environmental situation and finding creative ways to produce more than enough for you and the other person.

If you want to accurately understand behavior and why other people are not doing what you want, it is important to understand that people think and therefore act from different levels of ability.

Contrary to popular practice, it is to your advantage to help the other person feel more powerful rather than putting him under your thumb. As he feels safer, his thinking expands and you stand a better chance of having an adult to negotiate with instead of a kid.

You, in turn, will have the most power and the most options if you can keep yourself in Generative capacities. Using the four principles and the No-Fault Negotiating Formula will help you do that more often.

YOU START HERE

1. Start by taking the pressure off yourself and by making it as simple and easy as possible. You have a right to practice. Start with easy people in safe situations. Don't start with Goliath.
2. Practice using the No-Fault Negotiation Formula as an analytical tool; practice running through examples of the five steps in your head or as a written exercise before using it to do real-time negotiating. Practice it until you can think this way with some ease. When you're thinking this way, what you need to say will come out of your mouth naturally.
3. Whenever you get blocked or stuck, STOP. Take the time to:
   - Pay attention to what is immediately, obviously going on.
   - Separate in your mind the content, the quality of the relationship, the process you are using, and the criteria for settlement you both are using. If you're stuck on the content, shift the focus of your conversation to one of the other three elements.
   - Take responsibility for your own behavior.
   - Focus on the underlying needs and problems instead of pitting yourself against the other person.

- Do what you can do to enhance mutual understanding instead of beating the other person.

CHAPTER 20

A FINAL NOTE

We gotta wanta. Knowledge and skills make it faster and easier for us to get what we want from others, but no amount of knowledge or skill will make us an effective negotiator unless we truly want to negotiate.

We know the difference in our guts between times when we want to beat the other person and when we want to negotiate. When we want to beat the other person, we have win/lose feelings inside us. We are afraid of losing, we want to be right, or we want to make the other person pay. We need to be honest with ourselves when we have such win/lose feelings within us. Sometimes the price, whatever it may be, will be worth what we have to pay.

When we want to negotiate, we are willing to understand the needs and interests of the other person. When we are willing to do this, we stand our best chance of getting what we want over the long term. We will not always get what we want when we want it, how we want it, from whom we want it—but we can always get more than enough.

APPENDIX I

EASY REFERENCE TABLE OF CONTENTS

APPENDIX II

PLANNING GUIDE FOR NO-FAULT NEGOTIATING

This guide can be used before and during a negotiation.

1. FOCUSING ON KEY ISSUES

What environmental factors are affecting the other person? Myself? What pressures or stresses are each of us experiencing?

What are the triggering events or behaviors that tell me I have a problem or conflict to address? What is the other person really saying with his behavior?

What are the substantive issues we are addressing? What is the topic of our discussion?

Does it feel as if we are working together or are we pitted against each other? Are we fighting or dancing?

Are we blocked from solving the problem?

Do we have a repeated pattern of problems?

Do we simply have a problem or do we also have a relationship conflict? If we have a conflict, what is each person believing, feeling, and needing?

What is the relative importance of the substantive issues versus the ongoing relationship?

2. Identifying My Needs

What are my current thinking levels?

Do I want to "beat" the other person or understand him?

What am I feeling? If I am angry, what are the feelings of vulnerability underneath my anger?

What are my assumptions? My operating beliefs? How do I see myself in relation to the other person? What am I saying to myself about myself?

How am I limiting myself—giving my power away?

What do I fear? What am I afraid might happen?

What is keeping me from going for 100 percent? From drawing my boundaries? From confronting the other person?

What is going on in my body?

What does all of this tell me about what I am needing?

What do I want from the other person? What do I want them to do to help me meet my needs?

3. Understanding The Other Person

What do I know about the other person's background, his/her past experience and what his/her professional ambitions are?

What are his/her current thinking levels?

What is he/she doing behaviorally? Is he/she forcing or withdrawing, gaming or bargaining, denying or accommodating, being superior or dismissing? Or is he/she open and listening?

Why is the other person using particular strategies? What is his/her immediate behavior telling me about her needs and fears? What are her perceptions? What is motivating her behavior?

What is preventing the other person from understanding me? From giving me what I want? What will it cost him?

What environmental factors are affecting the other person?

Who forms the other person's constituency? To whom does he/she need to look good? How might he/she be criticized?

What does the other person want from me?

What would make it worthwhile for her to give me what I want?

Are there multiple interests on the other side?

Who has the power on the other side? Whose decision do I want to influence?

Do I accept the other person's needs and interests as valid for him? Who is the kid inside his adult body? Am I focusing on the other person's behaviors or on his inner kid?

4. Weighing The Costs

Do we have shared interests in maintaining a future relationship?

Can I afford to understand the other person—to take her in? Do I trust myself enough to choose to be vulnerable?

Can I afford to not understand the other person? What will it cost me if we do not reach an agreement?

If the negotiation involves a strike, how long can we afford to stay out?

How long can we afford to run the organization without the other side? Who can fill their functions? Do we have qualified people? What will this mean in terms of the public's confidence in us?

What will we do if the other person does not agree to our terms? If they make public statements? If they refuse to negotiate? If they stall?

If we beat the other party, what price will we pay later on? How are they likely to respond?

Should I go for a one-time big profit, or is it more valuable to me to develop an ongoing relationship?

If I quit, how likely is it that I can find another position? What will I do in the meantime?

What will it cost us in terms of lost work time not to resolve this conflict?

How important to us is this client? Do we have the time? What will we do if they decide to go elsewhere? What can we do to replace their business?

Can I afford to burn my bridges? Will I need them in the future?

How much influence do they have in the community?

What will it cost us to recruit, hire, and train a replacement?

If we don't sell now, what then?

Do we have other options?

What do I have to lose by addressing the conflict?

5. Choosing Our Strategies

What can I do to help the other person feel safer? To look good? To make it easy to listen to me? To help expand his capacities?

Am I expecting them to understand my side when I am not willing to understand their side?

What am I doing that might be threatening to them?

Am I trying to prove I am right? Am I trying to get the other person to admit he/she is wrong? To justify himself/herself? Am I asking "why" questions instead of "what" questions? Am I using rhetorical questions to blame the other person in subtle ways?

Am I listening to the other person or preparing my defense?

What would be the best time to approach the other person? When would he/she be most willing to listen to me?

Am I being pro-active rather than reactive? Talking about where I want to go rather than where we have been?

Have I encouraged the other person to vent their feelings?

Am I communicating in ways that move us toward or away from resolution? (Am I blaming, scorekeeping, withdrawing, avoiding, threatening, deceiving, being vague, talking about the other person rather than listening, or am I being descriptive, using "I" messages, being specific and direct, searching for mutual goals, expressing my need?)

Have I stated my assumptions as tentative questions or dogmatic judgments?

Have I stated the problem or my needs before stating what I want (my Solution)?

Have I surprised the other person by not living up to his/her worst expectations of me?

Am I overwhelming the other person with my data and questions? Am I allowing him/her time to process internally?

Do we need to resolve the relationship issues in order to solve the problem?

Have we separated the problem issues and the relationship issues in our discussion?

Have we talked specifically about our relationship or do we keep focusing on solving the problem?

Are we focusing on our mutual and differing needs or on defending our solutions or positions?

Have I allowed the other person to see me as a person with feelings and needs?

Have I told the other person what I need and want, specifically and forcefully? Or have I expected him/her to read my mind?

Have I acknowledged the other person's interests and needs?

Have I been flexible about all the creative ways we can solve the problems and meet my needs?

Have I been supportive of the other person while being firm about my needs?

Am I focusing on what is immediately going on?

Am I sidestepping power struggles to focus on our needs?

Am I allowing the discussion to progress beyond the symptoms to the real issues?

Do I keep focusing on what is obvious? What are the core issues here? What do we need to attend to?

What is keeping us blocked? What could I do to get us moving again?

Do we first need to agree to negotiate? Do we need to reach agreement about the process we will use? Do we need to agree to fair standards or criteria before addressing the problem?

Appendix III

Checklist For Negotiating Blocks

If you get blocked in your negotiating, use this checklist to get it moving again.

1. What am I saying to myself about myself? Am I setting myself up to lose before I begin?
2. What am I saying to myself about the other person? What assumptions am I making? What evidence do I have for my assumptions? Do I need to check them out?
3. Am I playing "future catastrophes"? If so, what is the worst thing that could happen?
4. What can I do to make the negotiation easier for myself? Can I break it up into smaller steps? What would the first step be? What do I need to be able to take that first step?
5. Am I limiting my options? Looking for the one right answer? Have I brainstormed alternatives?
6. Do I need to take a break?
7. Have I focused on the other person's external behaviors or the underlying issues and needs?
8. Have I checked out my data?
9. Am I accurately listening or am I planning my defense?
10. Have I chosen to be vulnerable? Have I let the other person know what I am feeling and how her behav-

ior is affecting me? Have I made her feel my presence?

11. Have I gotten their attention? Drawn my boundaries?
12. Have I told them what the content is behind my anger—what my anger is about?
13. Am I clear about what I need? Have I made a clear case for my needs with the other person?
14. Have I specifically told the other person what I want him to do?
15. Have I addressed the conflicts in our relationship?
16. Have I given up too soon? Have I assumed I couldn't go back and try it again?
17. Is my timing off?
18. Have I overwhelmed the other person with my questions and facts? Have I given him enough time to think?
19. Have I failed to tell them what I'm thinking or what I have decided to do?
20. Am I making my space work for me or against me?
21. If we have limited physical resources, have I accepted that fact? Am I willing to look for solutions in which we can both get what we need?
22. Have I prioritized my needs?
23. Have I taken a long-term perspective or gone for the one-time "big hit"?
24. Am I being firm about my needs while being flexible about the possible solutions?
25. Am I paying attention to what is immediately, obviously, going on between us?

APPENDIX IV

THE NO-FAULT NEGOTIATION APPROACH TO UNION CONTRACTS

The traditional approach to union/management negotiating is for the union to submit its list of demands at some specific time period before the contract terminates. The company then responds with its opposing positions and the battle is on.

Even if relationships between union and management groups are normally good, the initiation of the familiar bargaining ritual causes both sides to fall into defensive postures. Each side assumes the other cannot be trusted, and data is withheld and used strategically to gain advantage over the other side. Both sides worry about looking good to their respective constituencies. The focus is on emphasizing their differences and on outmaneuvering "the enemy."

This ritual dance costs both unions and companies a great deal in productivity, profits, and satisfaction.

1. It often creates resentment and distrust which in turn create a spectrum of self-protective and non-productive behaviors,such as resistance, sabotage, passive aggressiveness, blaming, threats, avoiding accountability, and avoiding initiative.

2. It diminishes everyone's ability to solve problems because their thinking literally constricts. People begin thinking in concrete, literal, immediate, and narrow terms. They perceive fewer options for solving problems.
3. It sometimes creates climates of cynicism in which people on both sides lose energy and commitment because they feel disempowered and no longer believe that what they do will make any difference.
4. It causes individuals to disengage emotionally from the company. They fail to perceive it as their company and to identify their success with the company's success.
5. The company loses the creativity and knowledge of its work force in moving the company into the future. The work force loses the satisfaction and rewards that come from doing that.
6. The work force and the management team waste their energy pulling in different directions and falsely assuming that each other is the enemy instead of focusing on the competition and synergistically pulling together to achieve their common mission and goals.

Is it possible to change the traditional ritual dance of union/management contract bargaining? I believe it is. I believe you will get better results with less work by following the four principles of *No-Fault Negotiating*.

Traditional contract bargaining focuses on the defense of predetermined opposing *solutions* to problems and needs. No-Fault contract negotiating focuses on mutual goal-setting and problem-solving. It begins at the beginning, not the end. It begins with identifying and analyzing company and employee *needs*. It goes on to determine mutual objectives and plans of action (contracts are one aspect of those plans) that will allow the company the flexibility and resources it needs to be successful while at the same time responding to the needs of all employees.

1. Create A Safe Environment

It is often assumed that it is to our advantage to put others at a disadvantage in our negotiation. Not true. As people become threatened or pressured, their ability to think literally diminishes. Traditional bargaining practices cause most participants to think in concrete, literal terms, the customary level of thinking of elementary-age children. That's why their behavior is often childish. Do you want children deciding your future for the next two years?

Your task is to make it as easy as possible for the other side to cooperate with you and to help them function from adult levels of thinking. You want to negotiate with adults, not children.

- Children can't listen well.
- They misinterpret behavior.
- They think in short-range, narrow, literal terms.
- They are afraid of not getting their fair share and therefore are deceptive.
- They perceive limited options for achieving desired outcomes.
- They can't step outside their immediate experience very well to evaluate whether their behavior (the process/what they are doing) is effective.
- They find it difficult to make and KEEP long-term commitments.

What are some things you can do to help both of you grow up and act like adults? What can you do to make them more likely to be willing to cooperate with you? Two options you might consider are: Developing Common Data and Learning A Common Language.

Developing Common Data

A common practice in contract bargaining is for both sides to withhold data and to distort or manipulate information to their advantage. This, of course, causes both sides to distrust each other and to focus on their differences.

The objective in any negotiation is to reach mutual understanding and commitment. The only way this can be achieved is when both parties share some commonality in how they view reality. To do this, they must have common data to analyze.

Set up a joint task force to gather and analyze market data or to study organizational problems. Do this as an ongoing process, not just a fluke at contract time. If you are part of management, share all your financial data and long-term goals. Reach agreement both about where you want the company to go and what it is going to take to get there. This might just set up different attitudes, unless it is really true that the other side is inherently dishonest, immoral, greedy, and cannot be trusted. What do you really believe about them? What is cause and what is effect? What do you think they will do if you don't live up to their worst expectations of you?

Learning a Common Language

"Would you rather negotiate with someone with poor negotiation skills or good skills?" I would take the person with good skills any day. Crazy? No! Good negotiation skills do not mean the person is more clever or dishonest. It means they are more conscious and have more confidence so they can afford to act like adults. Remember: the bigger the bully, the more frightened the kid on the inside, otherwise he would be acting out of his calm adult strength.

2. Shift Your Focus

Anytime you are negotiating, you have four elements or agenda items to negotiate:

1. The Problem—the terms of the contract.
2. The Relationship—the degree of trust or distrust and any past unresolved conflicts.
3. The Process—the way you negotiate the contract.
4. The Criteria—the standards for a fair agreement.

Some rules to follow:

a. DO NOT make the mistake of trying to negotiate the terms of the contract until you have first resolved the other three agenda items.

b. First address your relationship. If there are past conflicts, try to get them resolved. Be aware of your own attitudes toward the other side—what you expect of them positively and negatively. Your expectations have a way of coming true.

   Since the quality of your relationship with each other is one of the key factors determining the ease and the success of your negotiations, give them the attention they need instead of avoiding them. You should be working on establishing authentic and congruent relationships all the time. Don't wait until contract time. It may be too late.

c. Next, negotiate the process—how you are going to conduct your talks? Get their agreement to try another way—as outlined in this appendix. You may find you need to do some negotiating concerning the process before you can effectively address your relationship. By first negotiating the process—the rules and procedure—all parties know what to expect. They will feel safe and will be more willing to participate and cooperate.

d. Next develop common criteria. Direct the process so you end up working together to create mutual goals and to solve mutual problems. Make the competition your target by researching and analyzing market data together.

   By creating a common vision and common goals and by honestly addressing productivity as well as organizational problems, you end up creating a shared investment in the future. This creates a new type of criteria: criteria focused on achievement rather than on protection from being cheated.

e. When you have agreed on your process and your common goals, and when you are working together instead of against each other, only then should you address the contract. How to avoid getting stuck at this point in your negotiation is addressed in the next two principles.

3. Understand Them; Don't Beat Them

The principle is to focus on defining mutual and different needs and problems. DO NOT focus on solutions to problems.

Every time you get stuck in a negotiation, it it because you are fighting over who has the right answer. The way to get unstuck is to refocus on the underlying needs of both parties.

Presenting "wish lists" or demands at the beginning of a contract negotiation process is an example of focusing at the wrong end—on solutions. This is a sure way to get stuck in pitted bargaining positions.

Instead of beginning with "wish lists," begin with lists of the differing problems or concerns that need to be addressed. Focus on what the common interests are that both parties have in finding satisfactory solutions to these concerns. And during the negotiation process, continue to refocus on analyzing and understanding needs and problems whenever you begin to get stuck in opposing solutions.

For example, instead of getting stuck over the seniority system, talk about the values and needs that that solution (the seniority system) is supposed to address—namely, security and fairness. Identify the costs to both parties and the genuine needs of both parties.

If you have been successful in establishing authentic relationships and are focused on created a common future together, reasonable agreements will naturally emerge. In doing this, be clear about the difference between wanting to lead them to your predetermined solutions and focusing on solving your mutual problems.

4. Attend To The Obvious

The fourth principle, ATTEND TO THE OBVIOUS, is to pay attention to and address what is immediately, obviously going on. Negotiation is a process of removing blocks. By paying attention to what is immediately and obviously going on, you will remove each block as it arises.

Attending To The Obvious requires that you maintain a conscious, multiple-perspective awareness. It requires that you not lose yourself in the process or allow your emotions to overrun you. It requires that you be consciously aware of the content, the quality of relationships (degree of trust), the process (are we working together or against each other), and the criteria for settlement (fair standards and the needs of both parties).

In Attending To The Obvious, whenever one of the elements becomes a block, you immediately address it so you can dissolve the block. If you are getting confused, break the content down into manageable parts. If you are angry with each other or not trusting, directly talk about your relationship and what you can do to resolve the distrust. If they keep getting locked in either/or positions, find a way to translate these into and/both positions. If you disagree on an issue, back off and reach agreement first on mutually agreed upon fair standards. Or if they are resisting being cooperative, find out what they need to be willing to cooperate. Maybe they need your help to look good to their constituency.

SUMMARY

No one can guarantee that you can always get everything you want. That is not reality. But you can get more than enough and you have a greater likelihood of reaching reasonable solutions more easily and quickly without damaging your ongoing relationships if you follow the principles and process outlined above.

INDEX

About The Author

Len Leritz has distinguished himself in the organization development field with the research, consultation, and training he has provided for business and labor organizations, educational institutions, professional groups, university programs, churches, and health care organizations.

Over the past 20 years, he has evolved a developmental model of management excellence called Generative Management. His system of organizational assessment, management profiling, and monitoring activities identifies and develops the levels of thinking and relating among individuals in organizations. This process is used to create highly effective senior management teams and professional groups, to develop management depth in organizations, and to improve labor/management interactions.

Mr. Leritz holds graduate degrees from the University of Arkansas and Seattle University, and is President of Len Leritz and Associates, a Portland, Oregon based consulting group.